# Does Everyone Get a Turn to Be God?

Is God the elected President of the infinite universe?

What about Equal Fame, Fortune and
Brain Power for Everyone, Forever?
Anyway, let's abolish financial stress!

## Nemo Tee Noon, MD

cover art by Louise Amelia Braun-Jameyson

Order this book online at www.trafford.com
or email orders@trafford.com

Most Trafford titles are also available at major online book retailers.

Printed in the United States of America.

ISBN: 978-1-4669-4618-7 Softcover
ISBN: 978-1-4669-4619-4 e-Book
ISBN: 978-1-4907-4563-3 Audio

*Trafford rev. 12/11/2014*

 www.trafford.com

North America & international
toll-free: 1 888 232 4444 (USA & Canada)
fax: 812 355 4082

# An
# Extraordinary
# Acknowledgment

Special thanks to Jessica Jacobs,
without whose expert assistance,
this book would not be possible.

# Contents

"And the last shall be first, and the first, last."

—Matthew 20:16

# About the Author

Nemo Tee Noon, MD, is a psychiatrist with additional background in biophysics, bioengineering and electroencephalography (EEG) technology. He has been afflicted with various learning disabilities since childhood and disabled with severe obsessive-compulsive disorder (OCD) since 1985. His two major learning disabilities are gadgetaphobia and general information phobia. He has also been diagnosed with bipolar manic-depression since 2007.

He is a graduate of St. George's University School of Medicine (1983). And previously, in late 1974, worked briefly (as a research assistant) on "Artificial Vision for the Blind," under the auspices of Dr. William H. Dobelle at the University of Utah. Dr. Dobelle is cited in the 2005 Guinness Book of World Records under the headings of

Medical Phenomena and the "earliest successful artificial eye" on page 20.

The author also won an award for "academic excellence" in EEG technology from Graphic Controls Corporation and has had six articles published in *Speculations in Science and Technology and Medical Hypotheses*. He also had books titled *How Everyone Could Be Rich, Famous, Etc.* and *How We'll All Be Equally Rich, Famous, Brilliant, Etc.,* Forever published by Trafford in 2006 and 2010, respectively.

One of his goals is to play whatever role he can in the conceivable implementation of brain-stimulation-mediated learning facilitation (LF) and work skills facilitation (WF), enhancement and diversification.

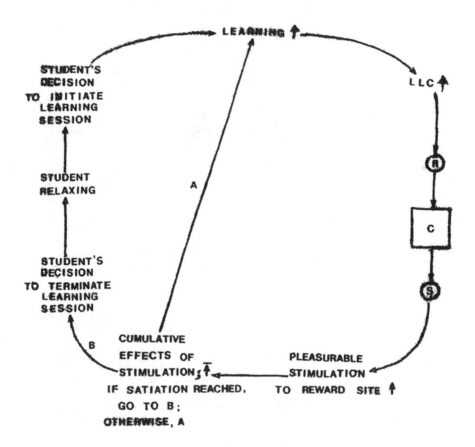

Figure One. Schematic diagram of how human (and animal) learning (and work skills performance) ability might be improved by a subtle variant or modified version of the psychologist, B. F. Skinner's operant conditioning (that is, essentially, a learning/educational-improvement paradigm that might entail instrumentally-mediated brain stimulation or some other kind of probably but not necessarily pleasurable and facilitative) mental activation. LLC = learning-linked characteristic, R = learned/newly-acquired response, C = central consciousizing circuit, S = (pleasurable) stimuli or stimulation.

A boy having his learning abilities and work skills improved and diversified by surgically-noninvasive pleasurable mind/brain stimulation. Cartoon, circa 1992, by Joani E. Wanecski ("Erica").

# Dedication

This book is dedicated to all of the following:

Nora, Dick, Douglas, Lynn, Christina, William, Sarah, Lory, Shirley, Tony, Herb, Lize, Charlotte, Ellsworth, Mary, Louis, Alice, Eugene, Grace, Isabel, Katherine, Jessica, Robert, William, Peter, David, Tom, Karen, Don, Donna, Deanne, Dom, Nancy, Maury, Ruth, Lisa, Byron, Trevor, Drew, C. Timothy, Akhlesh and Louise Amelia Braun-Jameyson

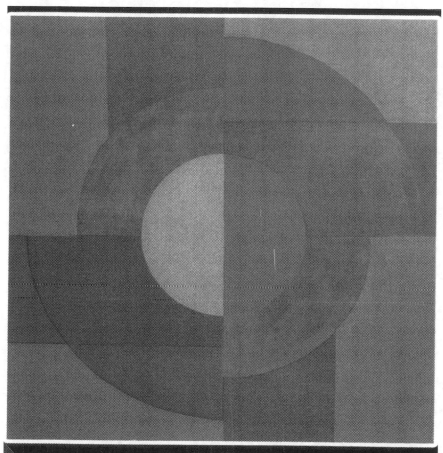

"Secret Center"
by Louise Amelia Braun-Jameyson
1986
Acrylic on Masonite, 28" x 28"

# <ins>Special Dedication to Louise Amelia Braun-Jameyson And Her Painting Titled "Secret Center"</ins>

Mrs. Louise Jameyson's lifetime here on planet Earth spanned from 1907 to 1997. But since I don't believe in death as an end point of consciousness, it makes more sense to refer to her in the present tense, except when reference is being made to events which occurred in the past.

I met her in 1958 in a context of her being head of the art department and the ceramics teacher at the grade school I attended between the ages of 7 and 17. She was friendly and down to earth, yet out-spokenly matter of fact, direct, assertive and bossy in a motherly, "Look, I'm old enough to be your grandmother" way. She was also simultaneously creative and *practical* about how to harness and take to fruition her own as well as any and all of her students' artistic impulses.

She was permissive enough to allow low-volume conversation among us students as we worked on our respective clay, metal or wooden objects of art. But she would raise her voice angrily and order us all to quiet down any time she thought the conversational activity had replaced the potential artwork as the central focus of attention.

I felt so comfortable with her (as though she were one of my elderly aunts) that one day, to my own surprise, when I was tired of hearing her tell us to quite down, I said, "You know what, Jamey?" (Her nickname is Jamey) She said, "No, what?" I said, "Right now you're just being a big jerk!" (She was always a rather large person.)

Guess what happened? She got up from her bench-seat, grabbed my left ear and led me to the door of the art studio, whereupon she ejected me with the following stern advice: "Come back when you're ready to apologize." I was so embarrassed that I told no one (who hadn't witnessed it with their own eyes and ears) about the incident.

I considered complaining to my parents, but doing so would have only led to conflict and unhappy results for everyone, especially me and my family. So, realizing that she was basically like a second mother and that my verbal behavior had been out of line, I apologized the next morning. And Jamey and I have been friends ever since.

So, to me, she is a specially good person. It seems I was the last person she spoke to before she passed on. Her last words to me were simply "Well, bye-bye, dear."

Although she was deeply religious in a "born Lutheran but converted to Roman Catholic sense," she never expressed any parthicular scientific (such as astrophysical) ideas or hypotheses that might have related to the interface between science and religion.

Nevertheless, the uncanny and highly coincidental title of Jamey's 1986 painting, "Secret Center," suggests that she was feeling and perhaps even thinking subconsciously along the same lines as I was feeling and thinking. "Secret Center" is a study in shades of red and blue that resembles or suggests a Christian cross superimposed over a moving planet-like orb that could be taken to symbolize planet Earth along with *the Lord's cosmically-center-stage sacrifice* superimposed over it. Hence, it might be interpreted as both a religious and scientifically suggestive work of art.

In any case, since the painting and its title could symbolize the human condition of *possibly* being center-stage to the infinite cosmos, despite our status as such being *actively* and incessantly hidden and kept a *secret* from us by an infinite horde of enviously angry extraterrestrial souls, it seems fitting that this painting should be acknowledged to have a possibly appropriate extended, alternate title of "Secret Center: How Famous and Glorious we Earthlings Will All Accurately Feel and How Valuable to the Universe We'll Realize Our Suffering Has Been When We're All Finally Allowed to Have the Truth about Our Center-Stage Status in the Infinite Cosmos."

Consequently, it is also appropriate to give Jamey, the creator of the painting, this special dedication. I hope you like it, dear Jamey.

# Introduction and Overview

dedicated to Douglas, Nora, and Bill

The first half of this book is autobiographic, because the things that happened to me motivated me to search for the reason why we're here on Earth. The second half is religio-scientific or, synonymously, theoscientific. The prefix, "theo" means "God." So, theoscience is the interface between science and religion.

Please keep in mind that this introduction is written in a heavier style than the rest of the book, which, thanks to the editorial transcription of my verbal dictation written up by Ms. Jessica Jacobs, is very easy to read.

Why should everyone get a turn to be God? There are two main reasons: (1) each being, animate or inanimate, is a self-creating particle who pops into existence spontaneously whenever environmental circumstances are such that it is more pleasurable to exist than not to exist and pops out of existence whenever it is less pleasurable to exist than not to exist. And apart from knowledge and wisdom, which are transferable from one mind soul particle to another, there is no reason to think anyone is superior to anyone-else, (2) if everyone didn't get a turn to be God; all Earthlings except God would be so jealous of God that we would collectively rebel and tear God down and crucify Him again and again, even continuously. This is what happens to long-term dictators on Earth, so why wouldn't it happen in God's case? The only sense in which God does create us is by assigning each mind/soul particle to a respective brain-body pair throughout its self-sacrificial lifetime on Earth (Hell).

As long as God is invisible, we don't feel too much jealousy toward Him. This is because, being intangible. He's not someone we can pin our jealousy on. If the same person were God forever, we'd get tired of Him or Her lording it over us and S(He)'d get tired of doing so by dint of all of the responsibility entailed by Her/His position and power. As Hillary Clinton once said in a Barbara Walters interview, "No one person should have too much power." Or, more colloquially, "Power corrupts; absolute power corrupts absolutely."

The main point of this book is that everyone, being a self-creating mind/soul particle, is equal not to something mediocre, but equal to the best condition, i.e., that of being God. Moreover, Nature (i.e., the spontaneous, mostly pleasurable force by which animate and inanimate objects, i.e., particles, pop out of nothingness into somethingness) would not be so unfair as to give virtually all of the power in the universe to one, two or three mind/soul particles and virtually none or relatively little to everyone else.

Nature tends to be egalitarian and equitable, at least in the long run, because there is no reason not to be. For example, for every action there is an equal but opposite reaction. In other words, "What goes around, comes around." This is basically the principle of karma, i.e., everything evens or equals out in the long run. This would apply to God as much as to you and me.

In a few words, if one mind/soul particle (MSP) were to have an eternal monopoly on power, the jealousy of all of the other MSPs would be so great that each of them/us would be so unhappy that it would be more pleasurable/less unpleasurable not to exist than to exist and all particles of matter (MSPs) would drop out of existence and you would have nothing but infinite expanses of empty space and time.

Before popping out of existence, the collectively conscious jealousy felt by all of the relatively powerless MSPs would be such as to foment a cosmic rebellion and overthrow of the one powerful MSP. Hence, with one and the same God forever and ever, you would have a universe so destabilized by jealousy of God, let's call it theoenvy, that the universe would be too chaotic and unstable to exist. And to avoid this cosmic instability, is the reason why everyone takes a turn exercising divine power, which, like the crown jewels of England, is/are transferable and pass-around-able.

One might argue that very chaotic and unstable situations exist here on Earth, but they persevere only because they are being stabilized from the outside by the infinite heavens. "God" and "President of the Universe" are interchangeable terms. In a universe big enough to have rivalry, hence suffering, only graduates of hell (who have learned to be compassionate) can run for the office of God/President or can vote for Her/Him. Otherwise, there would be an infinite number of ballots to count and an infinite number of candidates to choose among.

My accountant brother says that my notion that all of our pain and suffering is due to angrily jealous Extraterrestrials (who are upset because they didn't get included in centerstage Earth's resident population) is crazy. This may be "crazy", but its not as crazy as the notion that God permitted or even willed the Nazi holocaust, the recent typhoon in the Phillipines and all other pain and suffering. I still think the angry extraterrestrials force God to arrange all the planets and other heavenly bodies so that astronomers and astrophysicists mistakenly infer that Earth is just an ordinary planet.

My sister, a published author for many years, thought I had not adequately delineated why everyone should get a turn to be God. This introduction is intended to be more explicit in its answers.

A short answer as to why everyone should get a turn to be God is that everyone, being a self-creating particle, is intrinsically equal and, therefore, should enjoy an equal rank. The widespread portrayal in science fiction books and movies of extraterrestrials as being hostile to Earthlings may have a circumstantially rational basis after all. Hence, our intuition may tell us the truth about their hostile feelings toward us. And their ringleader is, of course, the devil.

Everyone wants to be the boss and to be famous. These are reasons why everyone should get a turn to be God. Why did Jesus have to be crucified? I say the extraterrestrials required it, not God the Father or humans except as they were influenced by the extraterrestrials.

Each person is an experiencer. What s(he) experiences is his-her experianda (knowledge, etc.). God's experianda (power, etc.) can be transferred to any other person. So, everyone could have a turn to be God.

It is extremely ironic that all Earthlings are famous throughout the universe but most are not famous throughout the world, yet. All of us are famous throughout the universe because God chose

Earth to be centerstage hell-TV. To be worldly famous, we would have to have the benefit of reproducible out of body experiences, so that each MSP (mind/soul particle) would be able to shed its cumbersome body and shake every other MSP's "hand" in order to be omni-directional friends.

God does not permit suffering. And free will does not necessitate suffering. After all, your free will could come down to a choice between and among various options, all of them free from suffering. If you do A, you could get apple pie, whereas, if you do B, you could get a chocolate sunday. Why does there have to be a bucket of excrement, regardless of how you use or "abuse" your free will? And if God invokes suffering because we're not worshiping and flattering Him enough, then we're saying He's as vain and trivial as many of us are.

God is extremely powerful, but not all-powerful and not powerful enough to prevent the Nazi holocaust and all other suffering. If God could prevent all suffering, he would surely do so. If He could squelch the devil and His extraterrestrial cohorts, He would do so.

Just because planet Earth is fraught with problems, pain and suffering, my accountant brother does not think that means its the center of the universe and hell. I say the extraterrestrial Earth rejectees/shut-outs, despite all their rottenness, are decent enough to put hell right smack in the middle of the universe, so that everyone can keep an eye on it both in order to be entertained by our suffering, which is a unique-in-all the universe marker, but also to watch over us to make sure circumstances and events don't get so bad that Earth destroys itself, in which case, the entire universe would be chaotically destroyed by dint of a lack of a central reference point by which heavenites could collaborate with each other and coordinate their intentions. Pleasure would vanish, and since outside of sacrificial planet Earth, all particles exist only because it's more pleasurable to exist than not to exist, there would remain only infinite but empty expanses of space and time.

Center-stage Earth, being so troubled and persecuted by the extraterrestrials, despite God's best efforts, could not exist at all, unless it were being stabilized by something much more pleasureful = stable, that is, heaven = outer space, where there tends to be no painful/effortful weight or learning/work related effort. In heaven (= outer space) work, learning, body building, etc. tend to be not only great fun but also effortless, but this wouldn't be possible without our painful, hence, attention-getting central reference point Earth, whereby heavenites can keep track of time and thereby cooperate with each other.

We know that if we're not interested in something (that is, if we don't take pleasure in it), it's very difficult to learn anything about it or to apply it. On the other hand, if we are interested in something, we can easily master the details thereof.

Theoscientifically speaking, someone or some group of individuals must have taken an interest in and mastered all of the structural and functional details of our world, because it exists in so much complex and intricate detail. Hence, intelligent design makes sense. Random genetic mutations would not have been enough to render our world in all its glorious detail.

Hence, intelligent design (as mediated by one or more designers) makes sense. However, this does not rule out either evolution or creationism. But survival of a species doesn't make much sense as a behavioral motive, because who says, "I want two children but, most importantly to me, I want to perpetuate my species?" Creationism is plausible because any time you or anyone else merely wishes you to exist, then you usually do exist. Your mind/soul particle (MSP) has a way of popping in and out of existence whenever you or a loved one wants you to do so.

Chimpanzees have 98.5 per cent of their genes in common with humans. Yet we can readily discern that the two species are much, much different. This points to the MSP as a greater determinant of our physical and mental characteristics than genes are. Nevertheless, all three methods, intelligent design, evolution and creationism could be applicable to our world.

To sum up, (1) everyone gets a turn to be God in order to avoid torrential jealousy, whereby the universe would be too unstable (via cosmic envy) to exist, (2) Earth must be center-stage to the universe, because there has to be something special and unique in all the universe (suffering) to hold the pleasureful rest of the universe's attention and rivet it on our center stage, central reference point or origin, $x = 0$, $y = 0$, $z = 0$. The populations of an infinite number of purely pleasurable planets have there attention riveted on us as the center of the universe, because our planet is unique in some way (i.e., being fraught with suffering). So, you may not enjoy worldly fame, but unknown to you, you're famous throughout the universe. Worldly fame, fortune and brainpower will come to you by the end of the cosmic suffering cycle, when all of our MSPs become intertwined or suspended within each other.

And the suffering-ful place needs to be kept in the God-chosen "center" of the universe, so all of the hostile, extraterrestrial heavenites can keep an eye on it to make sure the suffering doesn't destroy the central reference point (Earth). Earth is executed in such great detail that someone or some group of polytheistic Heavenites or some lesser group of Heavenites (who are steeped in their own interests = pleasure in relation to structural and functional details) must have designed it and continue to maintain it.

Moreover, the world is getting smaller all the time. The internet, GPS, etc. support this assertion. Sooner or later, once reproducible out-of-body, near-death experiences become readily reproducible, everyone's mind/soul particle (MSP) will be suspended alongside or within everyone else's MSP.

The collective consciousness everyone will literally feel will enable everyone to directly experience everyone else's pleasure, pain, wants, needs, and thoughts. There will be no more capitalism or selfishness. This would be utopia or heaven. There would also be no more laziness, because no one would feel hopeless, futile or angry about the polarization between rich and poor (which would vanish, anyway). I'm guessing this will happen around the year 2100 because of the rapid pace of technology and because 21 is generally considered the age of majority or adulthood. All past, present and future Earthlings will be part of this, because death is just an illusion which entails being trapped in a body.

Also, around 2100, all graduates of Earth (hell) will vote for a new God after Jesus returns, tells us we're all equal (including Him) and steps down from His highest of all possible positions. And the new God could just as easily be you or anyone else.

Everyone will be wealthy, famous and brilliant by the end of the 21st century, because reproducible out-of-body experiences will enable everyone's MSP to interact directly with everyone else's. So, everyone will care about everyone else's wants and needs, and accordingly, money will reflexly and automatically get redistributed, without socialism being involved. Everyone will be as rich as anyone is. Due to MSP-to-MSP contact, everyone will know each other, hence, we will all be world-famous. And we will all be brilliant because we will all have direct access to every MSP's knowledge. When all MSPs are in direct contact with all others, this condition might be called global collective consciousness (GCC).

When it comes to gadgets, I'm developmently disabled-due to a profound lack of interest in computers, etc. If lack of interest leads to disability and inability, then a less important way in which we might all be rich is via preferably surgically noninvasive brain (pacemaker) stimulation that will enable all of us to be interested in, industrious in relation to, and capable in relation to high-paying jobs. This technology will enable us to be interested in whatever we want to be interested in, even if we are not naturally interested in it. Let's call it brain-stimulation-mediated artificial interest (AIN), as opposed to artificial intelligence (AI).

# Chapter 1

## *Everyone's your cousin . . .*

First of all, everybody on the planet is a seventy-eighth cousin or closer, according to *The Guinness Book of Records,* so everybody is a cousin to everybody else. More specifically about my close family, my father's side was Italian, and my mother's side German, English, and Irish. My mother was a strong personality, and my father was easygoing but sort of distant because he was busy with his career as a general surgeon.

# Chapter 2

*I was very close to seven women—my mother, grandmas, and four aunts . . . .*

Basically, our mother raised me and my three siblings, but I was very close to both grandmothers, my father's two sisters and my mother's two sisters. I didn't really bond well with any older men as I was growing up, for some reason.

As I said, I have three siblings, and each one is a godsend in a different way. Unfortunately for me, one of my two brothers was killed in a car accident last year. My sister was like the homecoming queen: everybody thought she was pretty, she was popular, and intelligent too. One of my brothers was masculine, very athletic, and everybody knew that they had better not pick on me because he would pick on them. The other brother was the one who was killed in the car accident. That guy had a personality that would make anyone laugh. He had a very campy sense of humor, but still, because he was popular, he helped me. So the three of them all helped me.

As I said, I was very close to seven women—my mother, grandmas, and four aunts—but not to any older men for some reason. I felt un-masculine growing up. I was sort of confused about which gender I was, and I did enjoy cross-dressing until about the age of seven. I enjoyed wearing women's clothing until that time. The cross-dressing and gender identity confusion went away. I eventually decided that I'm just sort of soft—not really feminine, just a soft male.

# Chapter 3

*I had reason to believe that there were two areas in the brain for sexual arousal . . . .*

Also, up until the age of eight, I had reason to believe that there were two areas in the brain for arousal, one for gay arousal and one for straight, because I noticed that I would have two orgasms when I fantasized. Gradually between ages eight and eleven, my orientation switched entirely from being bisexual to being gay, and I wasn't happy about that, because I liked women better than men and, therefore, wanted to love women more, too.

When I was twelve, my obsessive-compulsive disorder began. My family and I were visiting Disneyland in Southern California, and suddenly I had a compulsion to swallow over and over again—anytime

I would think about the position of my tongue in my mouth, I would be forced to swallow. I told my mother, and she said, "Oh, you're probably just thirsty," but that wasn't it. It was definitely some extraterrestrial space alien(s) (Earth-excludee(s) or reject(s); (see explanation below), that had possession of me and was/were forcing me to swallow against my will. I still have this problem as well as an obsession-compulsion with psychosomatic hand-shakiness and another one with urinary and fecal incontinence, for which I wear an adult-sized diaper any time I leave the house.

Let's see, I was no good at sports. I was terrible in sports. Therefore, I wanted to be a brain, one of the gifted students. In terms of my high school record and all that, I was. I was near the top of my class, in both grades and standardized tests.

I actually had some minor sex play with another kid, and then I made his life miserable when really I was the one who had enticed him into it. So I felt really bad about it, and in later years I apologized to him. He accepted the apology.

I had a really close girlfriend in high school who I thought was the easiest person in the world to get along with. She didn't disagree with anything. She happened to be Jewish, and she went on to become a rabbi and a PhD in Eastern religion. But when she heard some other kids say that I was effeminate, she threw that back at me, because I hadn't called her all summer between eighth and ninth grades. So then I said really cruel things to her that can't very well be apologized for. I just kind of counted this as bad luck. It's too bad but you can't correct it.

I was also confused about gender, not just about orientation—I was confused about whether I was a boy or a girl. I worshipped these two brainy girls, Michelle and Hillary. They were both outstanding students, but I liked Hillary better, and she impressed me more with her portrayal in one of the Greek plays of "Electra."

I remember thinking in high school that I could be a good student in anything if there was some way of injecting pleasure into learning. After graduation, I went to Trinity College. During the summer of 1972—when I was twenty-one—I was sitting and listening to an organic chemistry lecture, and it was extremely boring. So I started dozing off, and then it occurred to me: if you could take a brainwave pattern that indicated whether someone were paying attention and then give that person pleasurable brain stimulation only if he or she were paying attention (as indicated by their brain waves), you could greatly augment learning ability. I told the idea to my lab partner, who was sitting next to me, and he said, "Oh, that's very creative," and I just knew that my life would never be the same after having that thought.

# Chapter 4

## *Around 1978, I met my future wife . . . .*

I kept getting medical school rejections, although I did get one acceptance to a school in India, and another acceptance to Grenada. In 1978, I met my future wife, who I thought was perfect for me, because she seemed to accept my orientation, which I told her about in advance. She said she wanted to have a family and children, but I told her I was too young. I was twenty-seven at the time, and this was 1978, and I felt I was too young! So I said, "Well, if you want to have a family and children, just come looking for me in six years." I said by thirty-three I'd be old enough.

Then she came to do an elective at the same hospital where I was doing my clinical clerkships after about two years. I thought she was perfect, because she wanted to go into psychiatry, and I thought she might buy my ideas about having an open marriage.

So I thought she was perfect because she seemed unconventional and interested in psychiatry, and her family lived only one hundred miles away from me in the United States. It turned out not to be a good idea, because she was actually in love with the traditional idea of marriage and family, and I wanted an open marriage and family. So things didn't work out. I felt bad, but you couldn't reconcile what she wanted with what I wanted.

# Chapter 5

*But that's the girl that I'm still involved with,*
*the girl that I met in 1980 . . . .*

My father died of pancreatic cancer before he had a chance to meet my late ex-wife. I had met a young lady in 1980, Laura, and she was extremely doting in attention and would call me ten times a day and send gifts. They were very thoughtful, and then I had to tell her that I was getting married to this girl who was going into psychiatry. She wrote a semi-nasty letter—it wasn't real bad. I read it to my roommate, and he didn't think it was too bad, but she obviously wasn't happy.

But that's the girl that I'm still involved with, the girl that I met in 1980. She is supposed to be coming here in March 2013. Even though she is a Republican and I'm a socialist, we get along. Also, I tend to be a very slow worker because I have high performance anxiety about most tasks, so in order to do any task, I have to surmount the performance anxiety. I'm like ten times slower than anybody else I know in doing any task because in going from task A to task B to task C, there is a huge mountain of performance anxiety that I need to climb. So that's why I'm so slow. Laura is faster than average in most respects, and it will be interesting to see how well she can tolerate my extreme slowness.

# Chapter 6

## *It was an acrimonious divorce . . . .*

I was in the psychiatry residency training program, and my ex-wife, Rosalynn, was too. I'm not saying anything bad about her. I'm saying that she preferred traditional marriage and I didn't. It was an acrimonious divorce, but I guess that's to be expected. I guess my daughter feels I abandoned her, so she's not communicative.

I didn't want my daughter to grow up in an atmosphere of harsh acrimony, so I said I wouldn't see her at all. I thought my ex-wife might be one of the supervisors, and I seemed to have some form of Tourette's disorder where, when I'm provoked, I can't control the words that come out of my mouth. Thus, I thought that since visitation would alienate my daughter anyway, it would be best just not to see her, but she took it as rejection. I thought that if she and her mother had financial problems, they would come looking for me, but that never happened.

# Chapter 7

*While my mother was alive, I didn't feel that*
*I could be a practicing gay . . . .*

So anyway, my mom died of alcoholism at sixty-five. My dad died
of pancreatic cancer at fifty-eight. While my mother was alive, I
didn't feel that I could be a practicing gay, because she was always
there, sort of providing financial stability in the background. When
she did die, I didn't feel that I could be active because of the threat
of HIV and AIDS, so for three years I just stayed in my apartment
and hardly saw anybody.

# Chapter 8

## *Allegations emerged that I had molested my daughter . . . .*

The allegation emerged that I had molested my daughter. I thought it very strange that a gay man would molest his daughter. I told one of my brothers about it—the brother who is extremely straight, the accountant brother—and he said, "Well, if you have one abnormality, the chances of having another one are good." That's what he said, but the judge told my attorney that I was too honest for my own good and I feel he knew that I was adamant, vehement and honest in my denial of any and all guilt in this matter.

I admired my ex-wife because she was more like my mother than my mother was and I have always had an admiration for strong women.

To me, she seemed like my mother, and so I thought, "They say that you marry somebody like your mother" Even though my ex-wife may not have been a perfect angel, you have to consider that I used to have temper tantrums and say all kinds of mean things, so in her mind she wouldn't be able to say, "Oh well, he's got Tourette's disorder" and overlook it.

To her, how I made her feel would be a lot more important than whatever diagnosis I might have, but let's just go ahead with the girl from 1980, Laura. She is very good, and I don't think that I'm going to meet some guy who is Mr. Right.

# Chapter 9

## *This time I am bonding well with an older man . . . .*

I live with an eighty-five-year-old guy born in 1926 whom I love as a person more than I thought anybody could love a person. He is twenty-five years older. When we started out, I met him at St. Louis Church, and since we're both gay, we tried some gay things, but they didn't work. He started having cardiac arrhythmias, so we just quit it. We're just friends. We've been just friends since 1995, and I do love him a lot. I'm just not attracted to him physically. I don't know whether he's attracted to me physically or not. Who knows?

So I'm staying here because I love the old guy. Remember when I mentioned that I never bonded with an older man? This time I am bonding well with an older man, so he fills a need that I have. My love for the old guy is enough to keep me here in Buffalo. So we'll just have to see what happens.

*This time I am bonding well with*

*an older man . . . .*

In other words, I live with an eighty-five-year-old guy born in 1926 whom I love as a person more than I thought anybody could love a person. He is twenty-five years older. We've had a father-son relationship from the get-go. And I'm totally satisfied with it. We met at Catholic Church. We're just friends. We've been just friends since 1993, and I do love him a lot.

# Chapter 10

## *My daughter doesn't know me, so it's hard to expect her to understand . . . .*

When I first saw my daughter, she was looking around like, "where am I?" She was a very cute little girl. She had a lot of hair and was the most feminine-looking baby I've ever seen. I thought, *Oh boy, you're in for a big surprise, because I believe this world to be hell.* I believe it's hell because our pains hurt a lot more than our pleasures feel good and it's much easier and faster to destroy anything than it is to create it.

As I've come to know her, she's kind of passive-aggressive in the sense of being unresponsive and ignoring my friendly overtures, but she might think that I'm passive-aggressive, because I didn't see her for 18+ years. Undoubtedly she was told that her daddy was given a choice to see her or not, and he chose not to see her. So that would make me seem passive-aggressive, but I'm sure she's a good person. I haven't seen her since she was four years old and she's 28 now (in 2012), and I haven't seen a picture of her since she was seven years old.

She graduated Phi Beta Kappa with a quadruple major in Italian literature, Italian language, psychology, and English, and the fact that she was interested in things Italian might show some interest in my heritage, because her mother was Danish. So I think she is passive-aggressive, but all I can do is to send her gifts periodically and hope that she gets them. I just sent her a gift, and I don't know if she'll get it because I had to send it to her old address. I even called an electronic voice, and it said it's undeliverable as such but may be forwarded. I'm hoping it will be forwarded. She should just give me her address. Passive-aggressive behavior consists largely in ignoring people in order to snub them.

I feel that she's passive-aggressive, and my sister was a little bit that way too. But, my sister has gradually changed in this respect. Sharil, my daughter, has the attitude that she doesn't care, so I mean, truth be told, if she ever needed a kidney or a liver or something I would be happy to give it to her, but she doesn't know these things. My daughter doesn't know me, so it's hard to expect her to understand my situation.

# Chapter 11

## *True Love will Prevail....*

My sister is a well-published writer. She has always been a strong and positive role model for me. She has always been interested in analytical thinking, mystery novels, fashion and beauty, the latter of which she possesses to a high degree.

However, when, at age 19, she fell head-over-heels in love with a perfectly likeable guy, for some strange reason, perhaps that he wasn't a doctor or a lawyer, my parents were so disconcerted that they didn't attend the wedding.

My two brothers and I received parental approval of our choices of wives. Ironically, our three marriages ended in divorce after 14, 16, and 3 years, respectively, whereas my sister's is still going strong after 45+ years. My parents did eventually come around and accepted my sister and her husband as a couple.

# Chapter 12

*Paxil has the wonderful effect of making me even less interested in anything physical . . . .*

If I had come out of the closet when my parents were both alive, I don't know what would've happened, but I just wasn't comfortable going that way. I don't want anyone to think that physical things are very important to me, because they actually are not, and this Paxil that I take has the wonderful effect of making me even less interested in anything physical.

# Chapter 13

## *I quit drinking because I got gastroesophageal reflux . . . .*

There was a period when I called up my ex-wife numerous times and said that I would have sex with her if she would let me have a relationship with Sharil. I was drinking heavily—I'm not an alcoholic in the usual sense, but I'm a chronic binge drinker. I got called to the city where they lived, to answer to harassment charges, but there was only a mild penalty. I think there was a fine of around two hundred dollars. I quit drinking because I got gastroesophageal reflux, and it's something I don't want to have.

# Chapter 14

## *Sharil seems apple-pie normal . . . .*

Having a daughter makes you realize that there is somebody who is, in a sense, more important than you are, because she will be part of the pre-utopian future. I'm part of the present, but personally I have a feeling I'm going to live to a very old age. She'll probably live to a very old age, too. I'd like to be part of her life. Even if I can't send her money or a copy of this book or anything else, I can always send her an e-mail, and she'll know that I'm thinking of her at least. I think that's important.

And I would've guessed that any child of mine would be as eccentric as I am, but she doesn't seem eccentric. Sharil seems apple-pie normal. When the parents have opposite characteristics, the offspring tend to be in the middle, so Sharil is probably normal in that she can keep a secret, at least as far as I know. That's what I would think.

# Chapter 15

*I thought I loved my ex-wife, but I didn't love her as much as I love the old man . . . .*

Salt Lake City, Utah, is where I studied bioengineering, biophysics and electrical engineering. And I had a good time with my friend Suresh the Indian. Suresh the Indian married my ex-wife's roommate, and they have two very bright daughters. One is like a genius. It's just ironic that my best friend, an Asian-Indian, would marry the Anglo-Saxon roommate of my ex-wife.

It's just a little aside, but when I told Norma—Norma is the roommate—that Rosalynn died about two weeks ago, Suresh tried to get through to Sharil, my daughter, to tell her my side of the story. I don't think he's had any success because I would've heard back from him, but we'll just have to play it by ear with my daughter. She may gradually come to have a different attitude toward me. I thought I loved my ex-wife, but I didn't love her as much as I love the old man. The old man is just—I don't know—just a loveable character, and it has nothing to do with anything physical.

# Chapter 16

*I've got this theory that I should've been born the heir to the British throne . . . .*

I've got a problem with attention, concentration and slowness. As I said, my slowness has to do with abnormally high performance anxiety. This seems to be my biggest problem: attention and concentration impairment. My current psychiatrist seems to think that my manic depression is as much of a problem as obsessive-compulsive disorder. He seems convinced of that. I, personally, doubt it.

I told him that since I'm a guy with megalomaniacal ideas, I should've been born into a place where megalomaniacal ideas would become everybody's knowledge. I've got this theory that I should've been born the heir to the British throne, and that way whatever ideas I might have, everybody in the world would know about them right away—like the guy at Medtronic Corporation.

I explained the immortality machine involving the puppy dogs to him, and he said, "Well, it's very interesting, but that's really out there. It's not something we're going to investigate, but I hope you're right."

My psychiatrist quoted me as saying I'm a savant. I don't think I said that, but maybe I did on a given day. It's more that I might be a low-grade savant, which is a person who is usually below-average in IQ but has islands of brilliance. I have an above-average IQ, but I might have islands of brightness. I wouldn't go so far as to say brilliance.

I said to my psychiatrist, "Couldn't the diagnosis be obsessive-compulsive disorder with mixed personality disorder with avoidant and narcissistic features?" And he said, "No, no, you're more clearly obsessive-compulsive disorder with manic depression." He says I sound more manic than anything else.

But this obsession with the British royal family is something that I've always had, and it even led to a compulsive situation of buying jewelry for my sister and my ladyfriend from 1980, Laura, starting in 2000. If I were in Prince Charlie's circumstances, then my women would be surrounded with baubles of all sorts, right? That's a rhetorical question, of course.

One of my aunts, my mother's sister Dorothy, looked like the queen of England, and they used to call her "Queeney" at the unemployment office where she worked in Arcade, New York. My sister, before she gained 30 pounds, she looked like Princess Diana, but I don't look anything like Charlie. I don't think my ex-wife or Laura would have had any interest if I did.

I have this obsession that I should've born into a circle where whatever I write about, the whole world would know about it tomorrow. You could say a lot of people would want that, and maybe so, but in the world in which we live right now, not everybody can be famous. The reason why not everyone can be famous boils down to the speed of light being relatively insurmountable—but, it's actually not insurmountable. So once each of us gets our mind particle (the essence of identity) out of our body, then all of us particles can move around fast enough for everybody to know everybody else.

# Chapter 17

## *So my thoughts are a big part of my life.*

Salt Lake City, Utah, was significant to me. I like that place, I enjoyed the friendship of the Indian guy, and I had a circle of friends. I enjoyed the place. Then I was accepted to medical school in India and had to send in $6,500, which was one year's tuition, and when I told them I wasn't coming, they refunded the money. So that was fairly decent of them at the medical school in southern India. One guy from my circle of friends did attend that college and married a female physician. I liked Utah.

# Chapter 18

*My family went on a trip to Europe, and it felt
like we were the British royal family . . . .*

I guess the first place that I liked was when I was nine years old.
My family went on a trip to Europe, and it felt like we were the
British royal family, because we were constantly being waited on.
My mother was a queenly woman. She was Miss Western New
York, and a screen test went with it, but she never went to the screen
test because she didn't want to be a movie actress. She looked a
little bit like a young Queen Elizabeth—not that much, though.
Aunt Dorothy looked more like Queen Elizabeth. I definitely have a
fixation on that family.

# Chapter 19

*I actually like Grenada better than Salt Lake City, because the people seemed so happy . . . .*

Getting back to places that I like, I like the island of Grenada. That's where the medical school is. It's a beautiful place. You couldn't ask for a place more beautiful than that. It's mountainous and covered with lush foliage. The people there are poor, but they seem happy. I actually like Grenada better than Salt Lake City, because—I don't know—the people were so happy. They seemed so happy, and they didn't have two nickels to rub together.

# Chapter 20

*The next job I had was at St. George's University School of Medicine in Grenada . . . .*

I had a job as a remedial reading teacher when I was at the Park School, and I enjoyed that. It was just two summers, and then the next job I had was at St. George's University School of Medicine in Grenada, where I was a psychology teaching assistant, because I received the highest score in the class on the psychology test. There were two other guys and I, and the three of us were teacher's assistants. My ex-wife didn't make the top three, but she was bright in her own way.

The next time I worked gainfully was in the psychiatry residency program, and because of my slowness, I was having a nervous breakdown—not getting enough sleep, etc. I enjoyed the work, but maybe if they'd been more supportive I could've done it. They let me go at the same time as my ex-wife announced that we were getting a divorce, so I guess they had been keeping me just out of deference to her.

So, she didn't want me, and they didn't want me, but I enjoyed the work even though it was maybe too much for me in terms of my slowness. In fact, I was given a job offer at Warren State Hospital, which is in Warren, Pennsylvania, but I felt stressed out. I felt as though I was having a nervous breakdown in Buffalo, so I just figured something else would come up. I thought psychiatry wouldn't work out for me, so I was pessimistic in this regard. I guess I'm more interested in writing than anything else.

Then I was in this electroencephalography technician's training program that was co-sponsored by the department of neurology in the medical school at the University of Buffalo and Niagara County Community College. We learned how to measure people's heads for electrodes. The electrodes would facilitate measuring the brainwaves, so technically I'm an electroencephalography technician—or to put it shortly, EEG technician.

A lady friend of mine, Genesia, and I won an award together. We both won an award from Graphic Controls Corporation, which was, at least in 1988, one of the leading makers of medical equipment in the world.

# Chapter 21

## *If I'm suddenly poor, I think I'll be able to handle it . . . .*

Right now, one of my priorities is trying to help people. For example, I'm trying to help my old buddy stay alive. His mother lived to be a hundred. He's eighty-five (born in 1926), and all of his siblings are alive. So I hope he'll live to ninety-something. If he doesn't, if I end up on welfare, getting one meal a day at a food pantry, I won't care very much because physical, material things aren't important to me. They used to be, but now they're not.

I would still have my interests including brain stimulation etc., but if I end up on welfare and getting one meal a day at a food pantry, I wouldn't be very upset, especially if I have some way of writing.

Because of my recently embraced belief that the world is hell, my standards are much lower than they used to be. I grew up in an upper-middle class family and everything about my life has been upper-middle class, but if I'm suddenly poor, I think I'd be able to handle it.

# Chapter 22

*Elaine was just absolutely the most agreeable person you could ever want to meet . . . .*

I have a lot of problems with the type-A personality. Now, my high school girlfriend, Elaine, had the quintessential type-B personality. She was just absolutely the most agreeable person you could ever want to meet. She was the mellowest person I ever met. She was the one who became a rabbi. I thought to myself, "Well, you will probably meet a lot of people like her." I never met one like her, not one. She was the quintessential type-B personality.

Laura, the girl from 1980, she's type-A. She has temper tantrums big time, so maybe she needs brain stimulation! Everybody, even within my own family—my mother, father, sister, brothers—none of them is a perfect type-B the way Elaine is. Elaine is still alive, and she's married to some guy, and so I ruled her out. I'd still be interested in her, because I never met anyone as mellow as she is.

You could say she's a "yes" person. She would nod her head in the affirmative to whatever you would say. I don't know what that says about me, that I would like somebody like that, but I've never known anybody else like her. Not one. Some have been somewhat close, but none in the same league. In any case, she's a really remarkable person.

# Chapter 23

*My mother's being an atheist taught me
to be an independent thinker . . . .*

My mother had the biggest influence on me. She was an atheist,
and that told me that not everything is as everybody else says.
Her being an atheist taught me to be an independent thinker.
She influenced me in that way. And then later on, in school, my
sister, Lenore, influenced me a lot, because she was just full of
energy.

I always kind of thought that since my sister is bright—with a high
IQ etc., higher than mine—my mother always felt let down by my
sister as far as Lenore's not really being a feminist. So I thought that

since I was intergendered, I could be the brilliant daughter. But then I saw Michelle and Hillary who were two brilliant young women, and I thought, "I admire them both." I admired Hillary more, because she was more creative.

# Chapter 24

*Hillary helped me decide which is more important, being creative or being analytical . . . .*

The painting, *Secret Center* by Louise Jameyson, comes very close to my theory that the Earth is secretly the center of the universe. She didn't have the same ideas or a scientific background. I said to Louise Jameyson, "What's the difference between Hillary and Michelle?" She said, "Michelle has a brilliant mind." I said, "What about Hillary?" And Louise said, "She has a creative mind." I said, "What about me?" She said, "You have a searching mind."

So that's the way she categorized the three of us. Hillary did influence me. Both of them had the lead position, the lead roles in the Greek plays put on by this elderly transsexual lady schoolteacher. There was a big fracas about whether she was gay or not, but actually it seemed that she thought she was a man in a woman's body. She had Michelle and Hillary playing the lead roles in their respective years.

Michelle stood stationary in the center of the stage and recited a huge number of lines, whereas Hillary moved around very dramatically, showing her athleticism and creative blend of physical and mental phenomena. So I was actually slightly more impressed with Hillary than I was with Michelle—more impressed with the creative mind than the brilliant mind. Hillary helped me decide which is more important, being creative or being analytical, and the answer, for me, comes down on the side of creative over analytical. If it has to be one or the other, then I'll take creative. On the other hand, Michelle scored higher on standardized tests, such as the SAT, than Hillary did. This may or may not suggest greater potential for achievement on the part of Michelle, as compared with Hillary.

# Chapter 25

*Everything would have gone a lot more smoothly if I had known how to keep my mouth shut . . . .*

I wish I had known how to keep my big mouth shut so that I wouldn't say things that I didn't mean in anger when I was younger. Everything would have gone a lot more smoothly if I had. Now I'm fairly mellow and don't say things that alienate people, but, I mean, not consuming alcohol is a big part of it. My eighty-five-year-old buddy thinks I need to quit alcohol entirely.

I think I can still get away with it. Like with my sister and brother-in-law or friends Mick and Katrina, I can still get away with it, but not too much—both because of gastric acid reflux, and also because I tend to open my big mouth and cause problems. So I think it's best not to drink very much.

# Chapter 26

*What inspired me growing up was the desire to be a brilliant daughter to my mother . . . .*

What inspired me growing up was the desire to be a brilliant daughter to my mother. That's what inspired me growing up. Despite the confusion about gender, now that I'm grown up, what inspires me is my observation and anticipation of the "smallering" of the world—the getting smaller of the world. Because I think that's going to happen. The smallering of the world is going to continue to the point that each person is going to know every other person. Therefore, everyone will be famous.

# Chapter 27

## *Those four people would qualify as the kindest . . . .*

The kindest person to me was the guy who was the head of the psychiatry residency training program. My medical school, St. George's University School of Medicine, was giving me problems, saying I didn't pass the final exam. I had a B minus average. And B minus was like above average, and C plus was below average.

So I had a B-minus average, and they were saying that I didn't pass the final. Dr. Karl told them that if they didn't pass me, he was going to create problems with the Board of Regents for all of St. George's graduates. So all of a sudden, they gave me another exam, and I passed. So he'd be number one.

The other three would be William M. Honig of the Western Australian Institute of Technology. He gave me my first published article: "How Learning Ability Might be Improved by Brain Stimulation". And then, David Horrobin, published several articles of mine in "Medical Hypotheses," including the one about the genetic engineering of a world without pain. Then, Akhlesh Lakhtakia, who published an article in "Speculations in Science and Technology." He gave me an opportunity to speak at Penn State University, too. He tried to get me to be a reader for the journal, but that didn't work out because I have always had overly focused interests. Those four people would qualify as the kindest.

# Chapter 28

## *I thought my mother was like a queen . . . .*

If anyone who has passed on lives within me, maybe my mother does. She had such a strong influence as I was growing up. I thought she was like a queen.

Mom and my siblings, at first, and both grandmothers and four aunts and to a lesser extent my father have been most important to me over the years. And then my best friends: Elaine the rabbi, Hillary the creative mind, Suresh the Indian, and Marty, my best friend at Trinity College. All had lesser but still significant influences on me.

So other than relatives, it would be Elaine, Marty, Suresh, of course my elderly buddy, Norman, and Laura (from 1980) who have influenced me the most. Maybe Laura doesn't have a type B personality as Elaine does, but she's always been supportive of me, even though she's somewhat volatile. So those are the people, as I said: mom, both grandmothers, four aunts, Elaine from high school, Marty from college, Hillary from high school, Suresh from graduate school, and my old buddy, Norman, who have shaped my psyche. Laura, too.

# Chapter 29

## *I was mainly not feeling masculine . . . .*

When I was growing up, I was totally uninterested in sports and interested in beautiful things, especially jewelry. I had this obsession with jewelry, and I would even put both index fingers to either side of my temples and point as if I were pointing at a piece of jewelry, even though there was nothing there. In my mind's eye, there was something there, and that sort of indicated to me that my mind must be a string, actually a string particle, because my fingers were pointing to a straight line configuration.

There is something in physics called string theory. When I was three or four years old, I wasn't thinking about that, but I thought it was very strange, the way I would point both index fingers toward a point in space where a piece of jewelry could be, but wasn't.

Well, I have had a terrible problem with wasting money, sending jewelry to Laura and my sister. It's compulsive behavior because while they like those things, they don't need them. They both have said they have enough to last them a lifetime, my sister and my lady friend, Laura.

I was mainly not feeling masculine. I was not interested in sports or in mechanical things. I'm not interested in mechanical things at all, and consequently, I'm very much of a novice when it comes to computers, because anything mechanical seems masculine to me, and it seems to fall outside of my radius of modus operandi. Sports were a big nemesis too.

Also, I had a sex-change dream once. I was eating some cereal and looked down and I was female. It didn't bother me; it neither upset me nor elated me. It was just matter-of-fact, and it only happened once, and I was very young when it happened, but there definitely was something about gender identity.

I used to enjoy dressing up in women's clothing when I was five or six years old, but then I got past that. When I turned seven, I said, "It's time to stop sucking my thumb and time to stop wearing women's clothing." I just made certain resolutions when I turned seven. I thought I was old enough to quit those things.

I have learning disabilities in connection with my lack of interest in masculine things, and a gadgets phobia or gadgetaphobia is one of them—meaning phobia about any gadgets. Then I also have general info phobia, even though on standardized tests I have done quite well in history and general information. I still feel that with ordinary day-to-day things, I'm not nearly as smart as other people are. I also experience practical phobia—like, I don't know how to cook a meal.

I remember, as a child, actually priding myself on being an intergendered person, and thinking therefore, "I don't have to be interested in the things that men or women typically are." Men are typically interested in mechanical things, and women are typically interested in cooking and domestic things, and so I thought that since I'm intergendered, I don't need to be interested in either one of those things. Instead I can be interested in high, ivorytowerish theories.

There is something—I don't know whether you ever heard of this, but it's called string theory. String theory says that all matter is made up of particles that are string-shaped. They supposedly have zero thickness, which is a lot of baloney, because nothing can have zero thickness. If it has zero thickness, then it doesn't exist. So let's just say a string particle has some slight thickness to it, and the length of it may be ten to the minus thirty-three meters.

But the fact that I was using my fingers to point toward a piece of imaginary jewelry sort of told me that my mind was a string and that my mind and my brain are two different things. The whole obsession with jewelry, I think, had to do with the fact that I thought that if somebody like me with megalomaniacal ideas were going to be born at all, he should've been born into the British Royal Family. If I were Prince Charlie, then whatever I would think or write about the whole world would know the next day.

# Chapter 30

*I called my daughter up, and she was quite upset that I had her phone number . . . .*

By the way, I spoke to my daughter for the first time in twenty-four years. I'm a novice at the computer, but I just happened to come across her phone number. I knew her boyfriend's name, so I put both of their names together and I got her phone number. I called her up, and she was quite upset that I had her phone number. Although she had given me her e-mail address, she said she didn't want me to be a part of her life. I said, "Well, if you ever change your mind, feel free to let me know." And I have sent her maybe five or six emails since then, but I wouldn't call again.

I know it was her because her voice sounded similar to my ex-wife's voice. Why bother her? But the thing is, she's got parental alienation syndrome, but she is functioning as an English teacher. So, let's just leave well enough alone.

However, I would think that somebody who's an English teacher and a writer would want to write about her experiences accurately. I can understand why she would feel that I abandoned her and I think criticizing me is certainly fair game. She has written me two letters. In the first letter, she said, "I don't like what was done to me." She didn't say who did it to her; she just said "what was done to me."

So anyway, I hope she is happy now. But I'm going to tell her, if she wants to write an exceptional book, not to write a book about me being a bad guy, because that's the typical situation. She should write an even-handed book, giving blame, saying what happened. That would sell a lot more copies than a book about just saying that I'm a bad guy.

# Chapter 31

*I sort of did become the brilliant daughter that
my mother always wanted . . . .*

But anyway, going back to my gender-identity disorder. I'm not all
the way transsexual, and I don't cross-dress in my adult life, but I
was fascinated with these two girls, Michelle and Hillary, because
they were both extremely intelligent. But I identified more with
the creative one than the analytical one. The creative one, Hillary,
went on to become a very successful architect, and the other one,
Michelle, became a very successful medical researcher.

And then there is my mom, who I was trying to please by becoming
a brilliant daughter, and I was a good student too. I mean, even
despite all my learning disabilities, I was second or third in my class

of forty, both on the standardized tests and on grades. The other two, the first two people in the grades department, had modest SATs, and the top two people in the SAT department had modest grades. I was high in the grades and the SATs, so I sort of did become the brilliant daughter that my mother always wanted. My sister disappointed her by falling in love with a married man instead of furthering her education, but she could have done both if my parents had been more broad-minded, tolerant and supportive.

# Chapter 32

*My mother wasn't a bad person,*
*just a difficult personality . . . .*

On the other hand, my mom kind of irritated me, because she was always right about little things. Like if she'd say it was going to rain, it would rain. It wasn't just that she'd get arthritis in her knees or something like that; she was just always right. When she would say somebody wasn't a very nice person, sure enough, it would turn out that they weren't a very nice person. So she was always right.

But then, in the end, she lost a million dollars to a woman who was a compulsive gambler. My mom was an atheist. And I didn't want for atheists to be right, and Mom was always right about everything, so I figured that she might've been right about there being no afterlife and no God., But when she lost a million dollars, I knew she wasn't right about everything. That had to do with alcohol, because being an atheist, God for my mom was eighty-four-proof scotch.

My dad was a general surgeon and he worked hard, and Mom was smart about investing their money before she got heavily into the alcohol. She was a bright lady too. She was bright in her own right. She was a chemist and a mathematician. As soon as there were four kids born four years in a row, she became a stay-at-home mother, but she was a bright lady too. My dad was bright also.

But she just didn't realize that alcohol could color somebody's outlook to the extent that it obviously did hers. She was lonely. Even though she had four adult children, she was lonely. She was a republican and I'm a socialist. I'm even a communist, to tell you the truth. I mean, not quite a communist, because I think people should be able to own property and take pride in ownership, but I am a socialist for sure. I actually want a "nanny state" and don't care about what anybody else's sentiments are.

But she was a really far-right republican—so much so that nobody wanted to talk to her because she was just such an Archie Bunker-type person. And when you'd engage her in a conversation, it was always like, "All the world is crazy except me and thee—and sometimes I wonder about thee." She was lonely because she alienated people. I mean, she wasn't a bad person at all, but she just had some kind of a personality disorder or something. She wasn't a bad person, just a difficult personality.

# Chapter 33

*I remember telling my mom that I was gay and that I thought men were better-looking . . . .*

When I was twenty-two, I told her that I was actually gay. I just wanted to talk about this briefly, because it was a little bit sensitive in 1973. But if Sigmund Freud could talk about it 100 years ago, I guess we can talk about it now. I remember telling my mom that I was gay and that I thought men were better looking than women. And she said, "No, if anything, women are better-looking." And I said, "Then why do women need to wear makeup and men don't?" And she said she didn't have any idea about that. I said, "Well do you perceive women as being better-looking?" She said no.

But then I went to visit a friend in Illinois, in Chicago, and there was a lady standing outside the theater. She befriended me and my buddy—it was just a straight buddy—but she was saying how men were better-looking too. Obviously I'm biased by my orientation. But I think men are envious of women, too.

Men don't want to see women in power, because men have what I call muliebrienvy (muliebria means female body parts), which means that men are envious of women because women have more sexually differentiating equipment between the breasts and the womb and multiple orgasms. So men are actually envious of women. Women are envious of men too, though, and Sigmund Freud's penis envy is just part of the bigger picture of my saying that men are better-looking.

# Chapter 34

## *My ex-wife really wouldn't have been a bad person if I hadn't brought out the worst in her . . . .*

Now I'll talk about my spouses, which doesn't include just my ex-wife—who probably really wouldn't have been a bad person if I hadn't brought out the worst in her. I had a little bit of Jekyll-Hyde personality, and I would yell mean things. I'm just saying I think the split would've been relatively amicable if I hadn't been mean in throwing insults at my ex-wife.

We had an argument in medical school in Grenada, and she said that these Cuban guys that she was hanging out with were saying that I preferred thin women, just as most guys do. So she asked me about it and I said, "Well, when everything is equal, I suppose I prefer thin women." But then she was upset, so I yelled at her. Then I felt bad, and I apologized to her the next day for yelling at her, but it was sort of like a preamble to what our life as a married couple was going to be, with me yelling at her just because she would have a little mood or two.

I said that I didn't mean the things I said. I don't know if it would've made any difference, but at least if I had never said mean things to her, then I wouldn't have any reason to feel guilty in relation to her.

# Chapter 35

## *Then I have a lady friend whom Norman's not envious of. . . .*

And then, my other two spouses—one is this eighty-five-year-old dude. I was attracted to him intensely as a person, never really physically. We did try some physical things, but then he had a heart murmur. Then I have a lady friend whom he's not envious of, because he doesn't believe that I'm at all heterosexual. He thinks I'm entirely gay, so he doesn't mind. If I were with some other guy, then he would feel as though affection was being taken away from him, but with Laura, he doesn't feel that way.

They like each other. I told him we might do something physical when she comes to visit in March, and he said, "Well, I don't care. I don't want to hear about it, but I don't care." But if it were a guy he would care. But anyway, Laura is expected to visit in March 2013 and she's very good. Maybe she's not Elaine the rabbi as far as being easygoing, but she's good in her own way. Maybe I need somebody strong-minded as long as they are not too strong-minded.

Norman has got two sisters. He's got many relatives, but he's closest to his two sisters, Leonarda and Isabel. And at first I didn't like them, because I felt they were like my mother because they are bossy and they admit they are bossy. But then I realized about five or ten years down the road—I've been with him for eighteen years (since 1993), just in a platonic relationship—but I realized that they are not bad. Maybe they are bossy, but you need bossy people to take charge in a world like this one. So they are not bad.

So for me to place them in the category of unfriendly people was really quite unfair and quite inaccurate. So Isabel and Leonarda are very much all right, and Norman is very much all right too. And I hope he lives to one hundred. Their mother lived to one hundred. Their father died of alcohol-related problems at sixty-seven, I think.

# Chapter 36

## *There is a lot of common knowledge that I don't have . . . .*

I have practical phobia—I don't know how to cook a meal. I don't know the first thing. My eighty-five-year-old buddy (born in 1926) does all the cooking, and because I'm not interested, I absorb nothing. Even if I'm standing there watching what he's doing to prepare a meal, I'm learning absolutely nothing. So there is a lot of common knowledge that I don't have.

I mean these theories that I've got might be interesting and all that, but as far as everyday things—gadgets, general information phobia and practical phobia—I'm in pretty sad shape. The only reason why I do well on tests of general information is because those tests are designed specifically to be gender-neutral, and they'll ask you things like about ballets and operas and things like that. They don't favor anybody; anybody who reads a little bit would know those things.

So even though I got a good score in general information on the medical college aptitude test, I don't care. I still know that I'm general-information-phobic and spatial-information-phobic. Like, when people stop me and ask me for driving directions, I just say I'm not from here, because why take up their time? Even though they are asking me to do them a favor, why waste their time?

# Chapter 37

*My lady friend thinks that Sharil doesn't realize that I didn't molest her, but I think she does realize it . . . .*

I would think that my daughter, Sharil is going to want to tell the truth exactly as it was, including saying that her father seemed to have abandoned her. I mean, she is an English teacher. She graduated Phi Beta Kappa with a quadruple major in Italian language, Italian literature, psychology, and English, but her main thing was English. Her mother was Danish, so in a way, it shows deference to me that she was so interested in things Italian. Her boyfriend is Italian too, I think.

I think that she's going to want to write about her experiences at some time. Those things about molestation never occurred.

Sharil is my daughter, and I want to believe she is special, but she is reacting in a typical fashion. By growing up and hearing nothing but bad things about me, it's understandable that that would color her perception. My lady friend thinks that Sharil doesn't realize that I didn't molest her but I contradicted her. I said, "Laurie, that's ridiculous." When she was four years old, she said these things only happened in her dreams, so there is no way that she thinks that I actually did them.

I mean, it would be a much more exceptional book if she could lay the cards on the table the way they belong without destroying anyone. I mean, my daughter was disappointed in life starting from a very young age (four years and ten months), and she was hurt. All right, acknowledge those things, and then say what really happened, and then say that you felt abandoned by your father.

So I would like to think that my daughter is exceptional enough to write an honest book. I mean, if she writes a book stating that I molested her, even though I didn't, and some such rubbish as that, nobody is going to look twice at the book. It's like, "Yeah, you were molested by your father, and sixty million other people were molested by their fathers." So she should write about what's really in her past. I don't know if she'll ever be open, honest and objective enough to write a book about what really happened, even though I am very interested in a truthful account of the relevant events.

# Chapter 38

## *Straight or gay . . .*

My situation in preferring or wanting to become straight has to do with my closeness with Laura. We're going into it with eyes wide open, because I told her I'm gay. If you know anything about guys, you know that any guy who says he is a bisexual is probably gay. I realize women are not quite so homophobic, in general. My surviving brother and sister are both incredibly straight.

If you ask women whether they are bisexual or what, many women will say, "I don't know." Whereas with guys, 98 percent of them, if you ask them if they are straight or gay, they'll be vehement that they are straight.

It's not the same with me. I'm going into this with eyes wide open with Laura. My perspective may be somewhat realistic because of my whole situation with the old guy and Laura.

Plus I'm interested in doing it in a scientific way. I saw something on television about people with Alzheimer's disease having electrodes in the hippocampus, and they are able to function again. Their Alzheimer's symptoms have gone away. And I told you about the lady with depression, and that they are going to be working on orientation too, because people should have a right to choose, to really choose, because a lot of straight women don't like men, and a lot of straight men don't like women. And some of these are the straightest people. So they should have a choice to be whatever they really want to be.

So, I'm in favor of that. I want to have brain stimulation, even if it requires an implantable electrode. My main priority would be to get rid of the obsessive-compulsive disorder, and then after that the learning disabilities as far as ordinary things, and then after that the orientation. But I just want to say that those are things that I would want to change if I could. And I think it's possible, and hope that these things can happen, despite my death wish.

My death wish has to do with feeling that I'm a misfit, and if I can get past that and if I have some kind of a job—I have been on disability since 1985, then my death wish might be less. But the psychiatry department was a little high-handed with me. They weren't totally wrong, because of my slowness. And I was having a nervous breakdown. So when my ex-wife Rosalynn announced that she wanted a divorce, shortly thereafter they said they were going to fire me. It was within a week's time of her announcement.

# Chapter 39

## *Sooner or later I want to have some kind of a job . . . .*

Then I got offered a job at Warren State Hospital in Warren, Pennsylvania, but I thought to myself, "I can't move away from my mother during her declining years," and I could see that alcohol wasn't going to let her live very many more years. She was in her early sixties. I didn't know any of this was going to happen with the false allegations or any of that, but I turned down Warren State Hospital.

So I haven't worked gainfully since 1985. I mean, I'm happy to be a companion to an eighty-five-year-old guy, a companion and driver to someone whom I love as a person immensely. But after he goes, (he was born in 1926), I don't know how I'll manage with the practicalities of daily living. But maybe he'll live, like his mother, to one hundred. I don't know. But sooner or later I want to have some kind of a job. I don't care if it's a government job. I want it to have something to do with psychiatry, but not high up on the list—a little more than a water boy.

# Chapter 40

## *We have an interesting family . . . .*

My brother Anthony, who is as straight as anybody and very masculine, an accountant—he's not creative, but he's had an interesting life too. He's had three wives. The first one was Jewish-Iranian and a very nice person. They are still on excellent terms and they have a son. The son, unfortunately, takes after our family, and he's got obsessive-compulsive disorder and attention-deficit disorder. Fortunately he is not gay, because that means less problems or challenges.

They're a very interesting family. Her parents were very wealthy to begin with. His first wife was not a brilliant student or anything, but she is a self-made millionaire. You can say it's her parents' connections, whatever, but the bottom line is she did it herself. It's not inherited money. Her folks are still alive, and I give her a lot of credit.

She and my brother, Anthony, fight over how much she wants to support their son, and Anthony is saying it needs to be a case of tough love, that they should cut him off. But Anthony's ex-wife won't cut him off, and I agree with her. I don't agree with my brother, but I mean, this tough love business is too tough. Maybe she has to set some limits at some point, but I don't think they should be as severe as what my brother is saying.

My sister is quite a character too. She is ultra-feminine. She's got an analytical mind, so she's not a dummy by any means. She wears all the jewelry I sent her. But it's time to cut out the jewelry and focus on writing, because jewelry will still be there but I've only got, like, four and a half more years to be on this generous disability policy. So I want to use it to the best effect, and frankly, I have been very impressed with Trafford.

# Chapter 41

*My interest in the brain culminated in a single moment at age twenty-one . . . .*

I remember thinking in high school that I could be a good student in anything if there was some way of injecting pleasure into learning, and shortly after having this thought, I went to Trinity College. During the summer of 1972—when I was twenty-one—I was sitting and listening to an organic chemistry lecture, and it was extremely boring. So I started dozing off, and then it occurred to me: if you could take a brainwave pattern that indicated whether someone were paying attention and then give that person pleasurable brain stimulation only if he or she were paying attention as indicated by the attention-specific brain wave pattern, you could greatly augment learning ability. I told the idea to my lab partner, who was sitting next to me, and he said, "Oh, that's very creative," and I just knew that my life would never be the same after having that thought.

My interest in the brain escalated in this first moment at age twenty-one when I thought of how to improve learning abilities, but then I didn't get into medical school. I submitted about 170 applications, but my grades were mediocre because I kind of goofed off during college. So I thought I'd write to either Robert Heath at Tulane University or William Dobelle at the University of Utah. I chose to write to Dobelle, because he was working on artificial vision for the blind using brain stimulation, whereas Heath, who was working on issues closer to psychiatry, and might've been, I thought, more likely to steal what I considered my learning idea.

I worked for William Dobelle on artificial vision for the blind. That didn't last long, because I wasn't any good at surgery, and he wanted me to operate on cats and implant electrodes. At first I'd been warned that he was a difficult personality. So it only lasted about three weeks before I quit.

He was in the *Guinness Book of World Records 2005* for the first successful artificial eye. It involved implants over the visual cortex on the brain and cameras in a pair of eyeglasses that would send images to those electrodes. He wasn't a bad guy, but I could tell he was just too cranky for me to work with.

So instead I went to the University of Utah, and there I had one close friend, an Indian friend, Suresh. I told him I was doing research in the library trying to find out whether or not anyone had tried to cure homosexuality, and some guy in Germany had actually tried it by making lesions in the brain, so I told my friend Suresh about it and he lent me some money and then I got money from my parents too and I just told them I was going to a psycho-surgeons' conference.

I had already told my mother I was gay, but I didn't want to tell my father, because I thought it would be more difficult for him to handle. In the summer of 1976, I went to Germany to speak with this guy, a doctor himself, who had been arrested for picking up teenagers in local bars. He had had this brain surgery, and he said his libido was much less afterward. But then the doctor who was the head of the project said he would have to talk to my father before he could do an operation on me. I thought it would kill my father if he knew what this was about, so I figured I'd just have to live with it.

# Chapter 42

*The second eureka moment came . . . .*

My first eureka moment was about the learning theory, and the second eureka moment came when I wrote an article that I also got published: "Riley-Day Syndrome, Brain Stimulation and the Genetic Engineering of a World without Pain." I thought about how to genetically engineer people so that they would feel pleasure most of the time and only feel an absence of pleasure when they were in any kind of physical danger, and I wondered why evolution wouldn't have taken that course.

There is a condition called Riley-Day syndrome, found mostly in Ashkenazi Jewish people, which causes an inability to feel pain. It's a dangerous condition, because those afflicted tend to chew off their tongues and things like that. But I'm saying that you could rig the system so that the person would get pleasure most of the time and simply lack a sensation of pleasure if they put their hand on a hot stove. Anyway, that was my second eureka moment.

# Chapter 43

*I've read that human beings prefer brain
stimulation arousal over sex . . . .*

Robert G. Heath and Charles E. Moan did a study in 1972 with
implanted electrodes in the septal area, which I gather is near
the hypothalamus. They took a nineteen-year-old gay man and
stimulated his septal region, then procured a prostitute from the
streets of New Orleans and paid her fifty dollars. She said that the
gay guy was the best time she'd ever had with anybody. Robert
Heath was criticized for even doing the study, but I've read that
human beings prefer brain stimulation arousal over actual sex—so
you could cure homosexuality, heterosexuality or pedophilia. You
could cure any sexual entity. If people prefer the pleasure of brain

stimulation over any type of interaction with another creature, then you can cure anything, sexually-speaking. So I'm kind of interested in that.

# Chapter 44

*I'm concerned about pleasing Laura;*
*it's just being as I am . . . .*

I don't want to lead Laura on too much, because maybe I will someday find some guy who is just right, but we have had this relationship for thirty years. There is a medication that I take, an anti-depressant called Paxil, that makes me totally uninterested in things physical, but after I talked to my psychiatrist and my medical doctor, I decided that when Laura comes to visit, I want to get off of the Paxil for a couple of months beforehand and take Viagra instead. I am concerned about pleasing her; it's just a question of being as I am . . . gay.

I wasn't born gay, because I was equally bisexual until the age of eight and conscious of that, but I became totally gay, even though

I got married and all that. So I'm interested in seeing the work of Robert Heath and Charles Moan replicated. Most of the studies on brain stimulation that I've seen didn't find the intense pleasure that Heath and Moan did.

# Chapter 45

*The third eureka idea was that the mind must be a particle . . . .*

So I'm wondering if Heath and Moan were actually stimulating the mind as opposed to the brain. The brain might be a relatively unresponsive thing, and the mind might be something different. If you think a person is being selfish, then how many things is that person concerned with? The answer is just one thing, which tells you that the self is a single entity. And if the self is a single entity, then it makes sense that it's a particle of some kind. However, if that particle of matter or, equivalently, a particle of energy can pop in and out of existence, then it can also change in size and shape, so a particle could grow to an infinite size and take any shape it wants. This particle of matter (which is the self and the essence of identity) is virtually synonymously a particle or bolus of energy, because matter and energy are interconvertible ($e=mc^2$). In other words matter is condensed energy and energy is dissolved matter.

So, the first two eureka ideas were the learning idea and the Riley-Day idea to take suffering away, and the third idea was that the mind must be a particle or morsel of matter/energy. Hence, you (your self) are a mind particle (MP), a soul particle (SP) or, synonymously a mind-soul particle (MSP) or mind-soul morsel (MSM).

# Chapter 46

*I would much prefer a noninvasive method,*
*like focused ultrasound . . . .*

The fourth idea was that you could take puppy dogs and put electrodes in the parietal lobe, gyrus angularis, and another electrode in a pleasure center that goes along with relaxation and sleep, and design a circuit with an external feedback loop so that the only way the puppy can get pleasurable brain stimulation is if its vital signs go away—its brainwaves, its EKG, and its pulse. If you were to switch the circuit so that the only way the puppy would get the pleasurable stimulation would be if the vital signs return, that would be an immortality machine in a nutshell. I've been in touch with people at Medtronic Corporation, and they've been very helpful. They said, though, to let them know when I am ready to leave Buffalo so that I might possibly be involved in a study, either as a researcher or, more probably, as an experimental subject or "guinea pig", but for now they have no additional studies planned.

Deep brain stimulation (DBS) is FDA-approved, for treatment of dystonia, which is a movement disorder, Parkinson's and essential tremor (uncontrollable shaking of the hands). But it's also an experimental treatment for obsessive-compulsive disorder, which I have, and depression, which I also have, and several other neuropsychiatric disorders. I would prefer to have something that's not invasive, because with invasive electrodes you have the dangers of hemorrhaging, scarring, hallucinations, and stroke.

But there are some people doing work using focused ultrasound. And they are using magnetic resonance imaging to visualize the structures inside the brain. They are using focused ultrasound to stimulate the structures in the brain, and as with implants, they are starting with Parkinson's disease, because Parkinson's disease is neurological but has psychological overtones.

Partly for Laura's sake, I would have implants. But I kind of bleed easily—I can't take aspirin. My blood seems to be thin, so I would much prefer a noninvasive method like the focused ultrasound. The other parts of my motivation in wanting to switch from being gay to straight are (a) a desire to be part of a cause and purpose bigger than myself and (b) an altruistic desire to give everyone a genuine choice of sexual orientation.

# Chapter 47

*The mind particles of the dead and the unborn are simply not imprisoned within bodies . . . .*

If everybody is just a particle, trapped inside a brain-body pair, then you could hold the whole human race in your hand. It would be just like a bunch of particles of sand, each one interacting with all the others. Everybody would know everybody else, so everybody would be famous.

Also, if we consider past and future earthlings, I believe that the mind-soul particles of the dead and the unborn are simply not imprisoned within bodies. I believe that you and I are imprisoned within bodies because the universe actually centers around Earth, and the infinite number of mind/soul particles in the universe are envious of our being center stage and don't want us to know it. So they force God, which I believe to be an elected position, to keep it from us as a secret.

Part of my belief is that our planet Earth is hell, because it's the center of the universe, and in order for the infinite number of soul particles to tolerate our being center stage, we have to put up with a lot of limitations and problems. The infinite number of soul particles are actually amused by our limitations and problems. God is not all-powerful, because if God were all-powerful, he wouldn't have let the Holocaust happen. If he could've prevented that, he wouldn't have let that or anything like it happen. If S(He) were all-powerful, S(He) wouldn't let suffering exist at all.

I feel that the Earth is at the center of the universe and the rest of the universe is envious. They make our lives hell in order to tolerate us being center stage, but each one of us is actually infinitely famous throughout the infinite universe—not within the world, but outside of it, we're infinitely famous. So they are jealous of that, and when we leave here, we'll be even bigger celebrities because we will have graduated from hell.

# Chapter 48

## *Everybody, I think, gets a turn to be God . . . .*

I don't believe God is superior to you or me. God is somebody who gets elected to be God, whether it's a trinity or just one or whatever. I don't believe that there is one God forever and ever and that it's always the same god. Most things in science are egalitarian—for every reaction there is an equal but opposite reaction.

So I guess I'm halfway between being an atheist and being a Catholic, because I do believe in Jesus and the other two parts of the trinity. I believe that they are the president of the universe collectively, but as far as the three of them always lording it over the rest of us, I can't see it. I believe everybody is equal. I believe that if your soul particle is immortal, then you could run for the office of God fifty thousand years from now and possibly get elected. In fact, everybody, I think, gets a turn to be God.

The other book I'm writing addresses in greater detail whether everybody gets a turn to be God, and the short answer is that everyone in the infinite long run of mind particle immortality has equal fortune and brain power forever. The even shorter answer is "yes."

# Chapter 49

*The past has been a history of the world getting smaller and smaller . . . .*

My life has taught me that the world is still a very unfair place and that the world is hell, and the farther you go back in time, the more hellish it was. I may be able to predict the big picture of the future because I can see the past. The past has been a history of the world getting smaller and smaller, progressively and communicationally. If you look at the human situation a hundred thousand years ago, there were pockets of population, and people in any given pocket of population had no way of communicating with people in distant pockets of population.

But as time went on, the world got smaller and smaller, communicationally speaking. And if the world can get smaller and smaller—I mean, if you want to call somebody in China or India, you can talk to them as though they are in the next room. So that's what I mean by the world getting smaller and smaller. And it's getting even smaller, because if you extrapolate and say the world is going to get even smaller, then everybody is going to know everybody else and everybody is going to materialize in everybody else's living room.

So even though some people who would say, "I don't want that," that's like people saying they don't want to be famous. I feel everybody does want to be famous, even the ones saying that they don't want to be famous. So I use the term *smallering*—the world is communicationally smallering all the time.

Two hundred thousand years ago, people couldn't communicate with people outside of their own locale, and now we can call somebody on the other side of the world and it sounds as though they are in the next room. Then, in fifty years, everybody is going to know everybody else, including the dead and the yet unborn, because the "dead" are just soul particles that have been separated from their bodies. They are not really dead. And the yet-to-be-born are just particles that haven't yet been assigned to be imprisoned within a body. You and I are imprisoned within our bodies.

Our bodies are relatively big, complicated things where a lot can go wrong, and that's part of the punishment of being center-stage. But anyway, the world is smallering all the time, and within the next fifty years, everyone on the planet, including the dead and the yet unborn, will know everybody else. So, all Earthlings of the past, present and future will be world famous.

# Chapter 50

*To me, it would seem that the world is a bad place, but it will get better . . . .*

The world is hell because, for example, it didn't work out for me in psychiatry. I had something that I liked, and it just didn't seem to work out. So yeah: it's just like I learned that the world is hell. It is also hell because everybody seems to be at cross-purposes with everybody else. It's also hell because there seems to be very little socioeconomic justice. Wealth, fame, brains and beauty seem to have more to do with luck rather than effort and effortful hard work.

Moreover, if in order to succeed you cannot be too nice, then that tells you the place (i.e. Earth) is a bad place, I think.

To me, it would seem that the world is a bad place, but it will get better. The world is hell right now, but I say in about fifty years, it'll be de-hellified and re-heavenized, and Jesus will return. He won't return to say that he is the Lord Almighty and always will be. He'll be returning to tell us that he's equal to us and we're equal to him and that we'll all have a chance to run for the office of God, and, sooner or later, everyone will get a turn.

So that's what I think. I mean, in the Old Testament, you have a God who is vengeful and vindictive, and in the New Testament, you have a kindly God, but he's still sure to emphasize that everything has to be his way. So it doesn't make sense. And then in the third book, everyone will be equal, equal to God, and everybody will get a turn to be God. That's what I think.

# Chapter 51

*Do you know how when you go to church
and there's a constant ideology of the eternal
supremacy of Jesus? I can't buy it . . . .*

I don't have the same beliefs that I was raised with. I believe everyone is intrinsically equal, and I believe that inanimate objects are different from animate objects only in that, with an inanimate object, the consciousness mechanism or switch is either turned off or only slightly on. So I'm saying that, like in the table here that I'm sitting at, all the particles inside that table are potentially conscious. So I think the difference between inanimate and animate objects is a very small one, i.e., a matter of the degree to which the consciousness switch is turned on. Both animate and inanimate particles are immortal in both directions of time. You never existed for the first time and you'll never exist for the last time. You pop in and out of existence for all eternity. And whenever you exist you can oscillate back and forth between being an animate and an inanimate object by dint of your consciousizer switch turning on and off.

When Yo're asleep, part of the time, you're an inanimate object, when your consciousness switch is turned off. So, you die a little each night, and return to full, animate life in the morning.

What got me interested in religion in the first place was asking my father, as we drove past a church that had a picture of Jesus in a stained glass window, "Is he God?" And Dad said "yes." So that sort of colored my view to a large degree, what Dad said. And I go to Catholic church now with my elderly buddy. It's near and dear to his heart to go to it, so we go. But I don't believe everything.

Do you know how when you go to church there's a constant ideology of the eternal supremacy of Jesus or of the Trinity? I can't buy it. I mean, I can buy that he's the current elected head of state, but I can't buy that it will always be him and him alone—because power corrupts, and absolute power corrupts absolutely. So that would suggest that God and the other two parts of the trinity cannot be the three elected heads forever or the one elected head forever.

I mean, it's like the whole idea of the trinity—they're one in the sense that one decision emanates from them, but they're three in that there are three different ways of looking at things. So the third part of the trinity ends up being the tiebreaker. So I just think that smaller universes might only have one God because they're less argumentative, being smaller, and I think there are an infinite number of universes and that the one we live in is especially large, possibly infinitely so.

And Jesus and the other two are the current elected heads of it, because with a larger universe, you need three of them for the sake of checks and balances. But with smaller universes, there doesn't need to be any suffering whatsoever. Nobody is envious in the smaller universes; everybody knows they're going to get a turn to be God, so that one God has less conflict to manage and doesn't need two virtual co-rulers.

# Chapter 52

*It just seems to me that everything
and everyone is equal . . . .*

Whereas in a universe that's infinitely big like ours, not every soul particle thinks that it's going to get a turn—even though they're told that they're going to get a turn, they don't believe it, because they've been waiting around for infinite time and it hasn't happened yet.

My ideas gradually changed when I was in Grenada in medical school in my late twenties and very early thirties. I remember thinking, "Well, if there isn't a God, there should be one." This is because our infinite universe does need a leader; otherwise you would have complete chaos, infinite hell and degeneration into infinite empty space and time. But this realization was still a long ways away from thinking that everybody's equal. Every soul particle is equal, which means every particle is equal. So each particle that makes up this Masonite table that I'm sitting at is equal to Jesus Christ and vice versa. It just seems to me that everything is equal, that everyone is equal. It just seems to me that that makes more sense. Why should nature favor one or three particles over all of the rest? Nature tends to entail karmic osmosis, whereby, although bad things happen to good people, worse things seem to happen to bad people, at least in the long run. So, over time, everyone seems to break even, with nature showing no favoritism to anyone. Karma, osmosis and nature, itself, are merely forces that derive their impetus from the collective consciousness of all inanimate (subconscious) and all animate (conscious) particle-beings.

And the fact that we have some people here on planet Earth that are way, way wealthier, more famous, and/or smarter than the rest, I think is just to make us feel the envy that the infinite number of mind particles feel toward us. They're not center stage, and they're saying, "Well, if we can tolerate our envy of you, then you can tolerate your envy of worldly celebrities." But I didn't think everybody was equal until I was maybe forty.

# Chapter 53

## *I'm a radical equalitarian . . . .*

I think that who I am at my core has changed greatly in the last ten years, because I didn't used to believe everybody was equal. I used to actually think that I was special somehow but couldn't define how. But now I'm convinced that every particle is equal to every other particle, so I've changed. I'm a radical equalitarian. Maybe that's why my current psychiatrist doesn't want to call me just a personality disorder, as the one from ten years ago did. That's maybe part of why my current psychiatrist would call me manic depressive and obsessive-compulsive (OCD). Maybe he's right—maybe I used to have a personality disorder and don't anymore—because that's not part of the diagnosis anymore.

I once said to my ex-wife, "You've got a personality disorder," and she said, "What about you?" I said, "I guess I have obsessive-compulsive personality disorder," and she said, "No, you're avoidant with narcissistic features." And then when my psychiatrist, a different psychiatrist, had to testify in connection with the false allegations, he said exactly what my ex wife said about my psychiatric diagnosis. I don't think that my ex wife and psychiatrist were talking to each other, so I think it's just what it looked like then. It's hard to know.

# Chapter 54

*Everyone is equal to God . . . .*

The two most important lessons I've learned in life are—1. Everyone is equal to everyone else. 2. Everybody is equal to God.

If I could pass down advice to posterity, I would say to treat everybody with the understanding that everybody is equal and equal to God.

# Chapter 55

*Outside of the scope of this life, everyone will play an equal role in the universe . . . .*

I'm most proud of my ideals. I believe that in the long run, outside of the scope of this life, everyone will play an equal role in the universe. This radical idea does not contradict the altruistic aspect of religion or most secular humanistic thinking. It doesn't. It doesn't contradict the loving aspect of religion at all, and it only contradicts secular thinking to a small degree.

People who are atheistic I find to be rather simple-minded theoscientically, i.e. religiously and scientifically-speaking. I've got one friend who loves science fiction, and he likes to go to science-fiction movies. Yet he believes that when you die, that's it and there's nothing more. I said to him—I don't want to alienate him—but I said to him, "How can you think that? Have you heard the expression that the truth is more fantastic than fiction?"

He said yes, but he still thinks what he thinks, which is when you die, that's it. I just think that's an incredibly simple-minded view of nature and that we have so many problems here that the world couldn't be as stable as it is if it weren't stabilized by something much bigger (Heaven). And also, the world seems to be executed in such detail that it would seem that somebody took pleasure in designing it, and we know it wasn't us. In other words, intelligent design which is pleasure-driven, has always played a large role in creative processes. So I just tend to see atheists as simple-minded, religiously and scientifically-speaking.

But I see rigid Catholics, for example, who believe that Jesus has an immutable monopoly on glory—I think they're simple-minded too. Anytime you go to church, all you're hearing about is how great Jesus is. I mean sure, he's a great guy, no doubt, but having everything centered around that one mind-soul particle (MSP) to me seems not as simple-minded as atheism, but still pretty simple-minded. And it seems to me that in the long run nature doesn't play favorites.

# Chapter 56

## *My passions are that everybody's equal and everybody's equal to God . . . .*

I'm passionate about my old buddy. He's eighty-five and all that, and even though it's not a physical relationship, I'm passionate about it, just because I enjoy being with him. He's not as mellow as Elaine was, but he's fairly mellow. He was born in 1926, but he keeps pretty busy.

And other passions—well, I'm just interested in playing whatever part I can play in pointing out that everybody's equal and equal to God. Those are my passions. And maybe I'll be interested in brain stimulation as an experimental subject or a guinea pig. I don't know. I'm not very good in the laboratory, so I'm better off with just writing. But it's conceivable that I could work in a laboratory at some point in the future. It's not inconceivable. But my passions are that everybody's equal and everybody's equal to God.

# Chapter 57

## *I think everybody should have a choice of sexual orientation . . . .*

I think everybody should have a choice of sexual orientation, a genuine choice—not be wired the way we're wired and that's that. It seems to me that people should have a choice. I think some heterosexual women would rather be involved with their best girl buddy instead of with a guy. And some heterosexual guys would prefer to be involved with their best boy buddy. I don't know, it just seems to me that some women and men are dissatisfied with the opposite gender, even if they don't realize it. In summary, some straight people might want to become gay, just as some gay people might want to become straight.

But in any case, everybody should have a choice. That's what I think. Except pedophiles—they should have a chance to become adultophiles (gay or straight). With brain stimulation, I believe they could be rid of their pedophile impulses. It's very unfortunate. I had a friend who was a pedophile. When I told him the whole situation with my daughter, he told me he was a pedophile.

His name was Albert, and he committed suicide. I sent some money over the years, but I was getting tired of it, so then I cut off the money. Later on, he killed himself. I spoke to his mother. He always said he was interested in children but that he never did anything with them and that his father didn't molest him. I don't know, but that's what he said.

But it was ironic that they were saying that I had done something when in fact I had a friend who said he would want to do that. When he came to visit me, I was careful not to leave him alone around my nephews. So what can you do?

It is probably possible to change anyone's sexual orientation via brain stimulation alone, but in order to change whether a person perceives men, women, children, etc. as being most beautiful, it may be necessary to use the methods of particle physics to change or modify the spin on the person's mind particle.

# Chapter 58

*Aliens are envious of us earthlings because Earth is at the center of the universe . . . .*

I even have an idea for an immortality machine, and I told it to the guy at Medtronic, and he said, "Well, I hope you're right, but it's too farfetched for us to research." But if I were Prince Charlie, it would get researched. So I've had this obsession that I don't believe God doesn't make mistakes. I believe that God is overpowered by extraterrestrial space aliens. And so God does not cause or permit suffering, but the extraterrestrial aliens are envious of us earthlings because Earth is at the center of the universe, and they are jealous, want to see us suffer, and force God to rotate us around the sun, for example, to make it look as though the Earth is not the center of the universe. So, our center stage status is being kept a secret from us, hence the appropriateness of Louis Jameyson's painting, "Secret Center."

But in reality, Earth is probably the center of the universe. It's just that the extraterrestrial space aliens who didn't get included in the earthling population are so furiously jealous that first of all, they took away all science, technology, and knowledge as recently as a couple million years ago and forced people to live in caves. Gradually, their anger has been subsiding, and begrudgingly, they've been giving us more and more science, technology and knowledge as time has gone on. Earth must be center stage because life here is a series of problems you have to solve. If the rest of the infinite universe were also problematic, then it would be too unstable to exist. Stability consists in pleasure NOT in problems.

So I have this crazy idea that I should've been born into the British royal family and that if it were up to Jesus, if it were up to God, then I would've been born into the British royal family. But the extraterrestrial space aliens said, "No, let him suffer. Let him be born into a provincial setting to an upper-middle-class family, but nothing extraordinary like the British royal family." The extraterrestrial space aliens are the mind-soul particles (MSPs) who were excluded from the finite population of Earthlings who were included within the infinite universe's central reference point (Earth).

So my obsession with jewelry has a little to do with the idea that if I were Prince Charlie, my women would be decked out in jewels. So it has something to do with that. And I'm still having that swallowing problem where if I think about swallowing, then I feel a compulsion to swallow, and I won't stop thinking about swallowing until I do swallow.

# Chapter 59

*In order to cure the swallowing obsession, I'm going to need brain stimulation . . . .*

I saw something on television just a few nights ago about deep brain stimulation and somebody named Helen Mayberg, a neurologist who reasoned that area twenty-five in the brain is overactive in depressed people. So she and a neurosurgeon went in and put electrodes in area twenty-five, and the person, this lady who had been nothing but suicidal for fifty years, all of a sudden started enjoying life.

Helen Mayberg and the other guy hold the patent on the device for depression, but there are people working on similar devices for what I've got, obsessive-compulsive disorder (and epilepsy, which I don't have) and a couple of other applications that I don't remember offhand. But anyway, I think in order to cure the swallowing obsession, I'm going to need brain stimulation down the road, and hopefully in five or six years they'll have something developed that's FDA-approved.

Helen Mayberg's area 25 may be the correct target for my obsessive-compulsive swallowing problem. Moreover, recently I learned that I'm not the only person who is obsessed with compulsive swallowing, breathing and blinking. There is a whole support group for people with body-focused sensorimotor symptoms which is based in Florida, under Dr. Steven Seau.

# Chapter 60

*I want a Dr. Kevorkian-style suicide or
I want a government job . . . .*

I also have a death wish, and the reason why I have a death wish is because I don't fit in with capitalism. I'm cut out to be a socialist. Maybe I'm just not capable; maybe I'm not smart enough to function as a psychiatrist in a capitalistic scenario. So I'm kind of hoping. Either I want a Dr. Kevorkian-style suicide or I want a government job where I'll do something in psychiatry, because I do have my four-year undergraduate degree in psychology and five years of medical school. Because I'm so slow, I spread it out from four and a half to five years. I didn't want to fail anything, so I spread it out to five years.

Then I did two years of residency—one year of internship and one year of residency in psychiatry—and that's when they fired me. I think they liked my ex-wife, Rosalynn, and I thought the only way that they were going to accept a "megalomaniac" like me was if they liked her. She died six months ago, of what, I don't know. But I had two years of psychiatry residency, so technically I've got a certificate of psychiatry residency, so technically I am a psychiatrist. Anyone who has an advanced degree in anything, even if it's not the full four years, is still a member of that profession.

So if I'm going to have a long life—I've got a ninety-seven-year-old uncle, and if I'm going to take after him, then either give me suicide or give me a government job that's something related to psychiatry. I'm too rusty to go back and learn all the stuff that I knew thirty years ago, but I could work as a screening person. Ironically, I would be screening people for suicidal tendencies, which you might think is like letting the wolf watch the sheep, but I would know that if that's my job, then I have to adhere to the guidelines under which I find myself.

# Chapter 61

## *So if we have no particular purpose, why can't we put an end to it? . . . .*

So I'm basically a socialist and have a hard time relating to conservative values and want a "nanny" state. And I feel that when people say that they want suicide, they are not trying to play God. I disagree. God is the one who's given us these painless means of going to a better place. So I'm entirely in favor of each person having the right to determine how long they are going to be here.

Atheists and existentialists would say that we're here with no particular purpose. So if we have no particular purpose, why can't we put an end to it? Or if, as I believe, we are here and do have a purpose, then we should have a right to self-determine how long we're going to serve that purpose. The purpose in question is connected with the possible reality that every fifteen billion years or so there is another big bang and every two thousand years or so an election of another God. But every fifteen billion years or so, in connection with the new big bang, whoever is elected God points his finger to a spot in the universe and says, "This will be the next center of the universe," and then everybody rushes toward that spot, because everybody wants to be center stage.

# Chapter 62

*Those extraterrestrial space aliens who enjoy*
*seeing us suffer need us . . . .*

I mean, that's just human nature. All the people (i.e. mind particles, MPs) rush toward the center-stage spot and literally knock their heads together, and that creates the big bang sound. But God does allow a finite number of organisms (soul particles) to live on the planet, on the central reference point, which during our current big bang cycle is planet Earth. But then everybody who's been excluded is jealous and becomes an extraterrestrial space alien, and they force God to make us suffer.

So, it isn't that God wills it or permits it. God is extremely powerful, but he's not powerful enough to prevent suffering. The reason why we're here on Earth is if the universe is full of an infinite number of planets with every conceivable type of pleasure, then the only way in which you can have a central reference point that stands out as something unique is if it has suffering. So, suffering is what makes our planet unique in the universe, and we're here to suffer, and we're doing it for the rest of the universe, as a favor, really.

Those extraterrestrial space aliens who enjoy seeing us suffer need us. I don't know if you took analytical geometry, but at the origin or center stage, $x$ equals 0, $y$ equals 0, and $z$ equals 0. And if hell didn't exist—planet Earth is hell—then there would be no central reference point for the universe. There would be complete chaos, and nobody out in heaven would be able to cooperate with anybody else, because you need to have a central reference point, spatially and timewise. How else could you tell time or specify a point in infinite space?

If you're a person (i.e. mind, soul, or mind-soul particle, MP, SP, MSP) out there in heaven but you're still envious of earthlings, then, you can say to a friend of yours, "Let's meet for lunch tomorrow at point $x$ equals 2 million, $y$ equals 5 million, and $z$ equals 10 million—and that's all with respect to Earth being $x$ equals $y$ *equals* $z$ equals 0. You have to have that, because the universe is infinitely large. How could the universe possibly have outer boundaries? And therefore, you have to have a planet which is arbitrarily selected, by God, to quantify space and time as the central reference point of the universe. Your purpose, as an earthling, is to entertain the infinite universe with your suffering. So, you're doing a favor to the universe, but you should be able to self-determine for how long you're going to do the favor. Remember, you are your MP (SP or MSP) whose incarceration in a relatively big and problematic brain-body pair is part of the down-side of the universe's tolerating your center-stage status.

# Chapter 63

## *We should be able to decide how long we're going to be here . . . .*

So our purpose here on Earth is to entertain the infinite, pleasurable universe with our suffering, but on the other hand, if we're doing a favor for the universe by being here, when you do a favor for somebody, shouldn't you have the right to decide how much of a favor you're going to do? You know, if somebody says, "May I borrow fifteen hundred dollars?" if you have the money, maybe you would say "yes." But supposing you don't, you have every right to say "No, I can't lend you fifteen hundred dollars, but I can lend you five hundred."

So it seems to me that if we're performing a service to the universe by being here in hell and entertaining heaven with our suffering, we should be able to determine how long we're going to be here, and for me, I'm sixty years old, (in 2012). I've had enough, and if there were a place that I could go to right here in New York, to sign up for a painless assisted suicide, I'd be first in line. I just think there are so many greater pleasures that await us out there—why wait around here being a martyr serving as a central reference point for the universe?

So either way, whether the atheists are right, or whether I am right, or I suppose whether traditional religious people are right (I don't understand what they think our purpose here is), we should be able to decide how long we're going to be here.

I had six articles and two books published. The first book was about how everyone could be rich, famous, etc., and the second book is about how we'll all be equally rich, famous, brilliant, etc., forever. Neither of these books is very well organized. I mean, I'm saying some—I think—reasonable things in those books, but I'm not saying them in the right way. I have a great deal of difficulty differentiating between what's important versus what isn't.

When I was working in psychiatry, my ex-wife would go home at five o'clock, the same as everybody else, whereas I would be there till midnight, working because I couldn't decide what was important about a patient or not important. So I would just write down everything, and it drove me nuts. So the same problems came into these two books. I'm not saying that substance isn't more important than style, but, if you don't have a good style, substance has a hard time getting taken seriously.

So yes, the six articles were well organized because they were very, very short, and people have been contacting me, especially about one article, "Riley-Day Syndrome Brain Stimulation and the Genetic Engineering of a World without Pain." People have been contacting me about that even now, saying that that's the first scientific approach that they've ever read in relation to abolishing suffering. Another article was "Brain Stimulation to Treat Mental Illness and Enhance Human Learning, Creativity, Performance, Altruism, and Defenses against Suffering." This one also generated some interest. Both of these articles were published in the journal, Medical Hypotheses. They were, respectively, Medical Hypotheses (1992) 31, 201-207 and Medical Hypotheses 21: 209-219, 1986.

# Chapter 64

*The self is just one thing, and it's got to be one particle with variable size . . . .*

Before we get into how everyone could be rich, I want to say two things. One is that the difference between animate objects and inanimate objects is tremendously small. Any particle in the universe, if you turn on its consciousizer-on switch, becomes a conscious being. Your brain is made up of zillions of particles, but your mind is one particle, and it has its consciousizer turned on. If there were two particles in your brain, both with their consciousizers turned on, then you would have the situation of two identical twins, even though you're apparently just one person walking around.

If you had two turned-on particles in your brain, that is, each with its consciousness switch turned fully on, you'd be in constant conflict with yourself. It would boil down to things like one hand removing your clothing and the other hand putting it back on, so it would be like conjoined twins if you had two consciousized particles in one brain. It would also be multiple personality disorder.

I did hear about a case of two young girls under ten years of age who are conjoined. They have two faces, but they have one brain. They fight constantly, because one is dominant and scratches the other one's face. And so the difference between the animate and inanimate is very slight. You could take one particle out of this table and turn on its consciousizer and it would be equal to Jesus Christ or anybody else. Mind versus brain.

When you think somebody is being selfish, then how many things are they concerned with? Just one thing. So our intuition tells us that the self is one thing, and if it's one thing, it can't be the whole brain because the brain is zillions of things. The brain may be made up of those super string particles that I was talking about before. Your brain and my brain contain zillions of those, but the self is one thing. It's just one thing, and it's got to be one particle with variable size. If string theorists are correct, and everything is made out of string particles, then your mind, being something, i.e. a single entity, must be a single string particle with its consciousizer switch turned on.

If that particle can flicker in and out of existence, then it can flicker from being small to being large enough to be seen in your brain to being the size of the universe. So your mind particle (which is you, i.e., your MP) has as its normal size, ten to the minus thirty-three meters and almost zero thickness, but it can grow to any size and shape you desire. Jesus is not the only one who can grow to any size—you and I could too. When we get elected God thousands or millions of years from now, then we, too, could grow to whatever size is necessary for the universe.

# Chapter 65

*So what you need is a device—a mind stimulator . . . .*

You would need to have a mind/brain stimulator that turns on pleasurable mind/brain stimulation when and only when, and if and only if the recipient's mind/brain is emitting mind/brain waves that specifically identify learning, working, attention and concentration. Okay, now getting back to how everyone can become rich. That's much simpler. First of all, you have to make a distinction between brain stimulation and mind stimulation. You might need mind/brain stimulation, not just brain stimulation, because the brain, itself may not contain intense pleasure centers the way the mind probably does. It remains to be seen whether or not the brain itself contains intense pleasure centers. Perhaps it does, but since the mind is the essence of identity or self, it may be a more likely candidate for subserving intense pleasure.

In a nutshell, the way to make everybody rich is to enable everybody to be interested in whatever they want to be interested in. Let's say you don't like mathematics—let's just say it—but you want to be interested in math because you know it's useful in science and technology. So what you need is a device—a mind/brain stimulator. We could call it a brain stimulator, but it may be more accurate to call it a mind/brain stimulator. In my first two books, I called every mind/brain stimulator a brain stimulator because that's what's going on in contemporary circles in science, but it's possibly more accurate to say mind/brain stimulator.

So what you do is you have your person equipped with a mind/brain stimulator, trying to read a book or something on the computer, and you could either have an implanted electrode, which I am not in favor of, or a noninvasive device that uses sound waves and electromagnetic fields, which I would prefer—that way you don't have to open the scalp or the skull. Then you just have the noninvasive mind/brain stimulator focus on a suitable pleasure center in the brain, and a suitable pleasure center would not be one having to do with food or sex because when we think about food or sex, we're not thinking about the kinds of things that command high wages in the workplace in general. Then you have an external mind/brain stimulator that only delivers pleasurable stimulation if the mind/brain is giving off detectable learning- or working-characteristic waveforms. And this approach will enable everyone to become very productive and effectively hard-working, because learning and working will become effortless, and intensely pleasurable.

So you have an electrode implanted in a pleasure center, a suitable pleasure center, or you have a noninvasive ultrasonic magnetic resonance imaging focusing device. Then you have an external feedback loop so that any time the person studies math, let's say, the person enjoys doing it intensely, by dint of the pleasurable stimulation. The student/worker would only get the pleasure if and when (s)he were paying intense attention (as indicated by their brain waves) to and engrossed in the subject matter to be learned, be it math or anything else.

So she or he all of a sudden finds it extremely enjoyable, and whatever it is that pays a lot of money or a good income—you just assign everybody to their self-chosen job, and then have this pleasurable mind/brain hookup so that whenever they are studying the subject, (as indicated by learning-specific brain waves) which wouldn't normally interest them, they come to be interested in it because of the pleasurable mind/brain stimulation. Everyone would be rich for two reasons: (1) pleasurable mind/brain stimulation would take the effort out of learning and working, so goods and services would become so plentiful that they would become free and (2) global MP circulation would enable everyone to experience everyone else's wants and needs as if they were their own, and, accordingly, there would be voluntary redistribution of wealth.

A third reason would be that everyone could become interested in whatever pays a lot, such as electrical and computer engineering, entrepreneurial skills and big business.

# Chapter 66

*Everyone could be famous, because each*
*of us is just a particle . . . .*

And now how everyone could be famous. Everyone could be famous, because each of us is just a particle. I've got a theory—I've got a mechanism called an immortality machine. You develop this device probably using puppy dogs. Puppy dogs are more human in the sense that they are more concerned about what we humans want than chimpanzees, who can rip our arms out. So I say work with puppies.

Just have an electrode implanted in a pleasure center, and whenever the puppy's vital signs—the brainwaves, EKG and the pulse—go away, that's when the puppy gets the pleasurable brain stimulation.

You would have to use the methods of particle physics to sort of trap the mind particle, but then you'd be able to flip the switch on the circuit and make it so that the only way the puppy would continue to get the pleasurable stimulation would be if the mind particle goes back into the brain and the body, as indicated by the vital signs returning.

So eventually it's going to become possible to have reproducible out-of-body experiences so that your mind particle can leave your brain and you'll see yourself sitting in your chair, your body without your mind particle. And each earthling's mind particle will just see their body resting somewhere, and will see everybody else on the planet, all of our mind particles, including the mind particles of non-human species such as puppy dogs, the dead and the yet to be born—because the dead are concerned about us just the same way as we're concerned about our ancestors, and the yet-to-be-born are concerned about us because we're their ancestors. So, the un-incarnated mind particles of both our ancestors and our descendants hover close to Earth, because they are interested in and concerned for us incarnated Earthling mind particles(MPs).

When this technology becomes available, the mind particles of all current earthlings (human and non-human) as well as the so-called dead earthlings, as well as the so-called yet-to-be-born earthlings, all those mind particles will come together. According to genealogists in Salt Lake City, Utah, where I worked as a graduate student for a while, about one hundred billion people have lived. I think the figure has got to be much higher than that, but even if we would say a trillion, then a trillion particles isn't that much when you consider that a bucket of sand contains anywhere from one billion to one trillion grains of sand, depending on the size of the grains. If you throw in all the mind particles of all past, present, and future members of other (non-human) Earthlings species, the number might increase dramatically, but not prohibitively as far as everyone being famous by dint of everyone interacting with everyone else.

# Chapter 67

## *Everyone is going to be brilliant, rich, famous, etc.*

Let's limit our discussion for simplicity's sake to human mind particles (MPs). If you have a trillion particles of sand, they can all interact with each other. You could almost hold them in the palm of your hand. The point is that all the mind particles that have ever lived, that are currently alive and that will ever live—it's some number like a trillion, let's say. And each one of those trillion is capable of rubbing up against every other one and getting its knowledge.

Learning is going to be so much fun in the future that everybody is going to speak every language, so there'll only be one language, and the one language will be English, Chinese, Spanish, etc. all put together. It'll all be one language, and because each mind particle will be rubbing up against every other mind particle, then it'll be possible for each mind particle to absorb the knowledge contained in every other mind particle.

So you and I and everybody else are going to know everybody else's thoughts as we know our own. We're also going to feel everybody else's wants and needs, which is going to entail automatic, voluntary socialism, because the reason why we don't have socialism is because people are selfish. The very wealthy are aware of their own wants and needs, but that's where it ends.

But I'm saying this will all happen with mind particle circulation—that's what I call it, MPC, mind particle circulation. So every past, present, and future earthling mind particle will brush up against every other one and glean its knowledge. So everybody will know what everybody else knows, and therefore everybody is going to make the people on *Jeopardy* look developmentally-disabled. Because if you and I know what everybody else on the planet knows, plus the information, concepts and skills of all the deceased and the yet-to-be-born, then everybody is going be smarter than anyone is now. And we'll all be able to scan the knowledge within each and every computer, and have that much more knowledge.

So that's part of how everyone is going to be rich too. How everyone is going to be brilliant is definitely there, and everyone is going to be famous because if your mind particle is brushing up against everybody else's mind particle, as if to shake hands—your mind particle might actually shake hands with every other mind particle because it has a changeable, variable shape to it—then everyone will be famous, because everyone will know everyone else.

# Chapter 68

*Your mind particle is ageless and immortal
and always has existed (and always will exist)
intermittently . . . .*

Your mind particle is ageless and immortal, because ageing is basically a process of something falling apart into its component parts. But your mind particle cannot age, because it has no component parts to fall apart into. Therefore, your soul particle (SP)—or, synonymously, your mind particle (MP)—cannot and does not age. When mind particles get tired, they drop out of existence and disappear, but your mind particle can come right back into existence when it's rejuvenated and gotten some rest from the stress of existence.

So your mind particle is ageless and immortal and always has existed intermittently, and it always will exist intermittently. You didn't need God to create you. God created you only in two senses: (1) by choosing you to live in hell, which is the central reference point of the universe and (2) by choosing the brain-body pair in which your mind particle will be imprisoned for a lifetime. It's like a movie-star was born, because planet Earth, as horrible as it is, is at the center of the universe, and each one of us is a movie star here, even though we may be anonymous as far as the world around us is concerned. Throughout the infinite universe, we're infinitely famous. So that's another paradox.

The universe contains an infinite number of mind particles (MPs), and they're all looking at us because we're at the central reference point. But in order for us to be interesting enough to be worthy of being the central reference point, we have to endure suffering, because that's what makes our planet unique. On every other planet in the universe, there is nothing but pleasure of every conceivable kind.

My old buddy Norman says they don't have sex in heaven. I say they do have sex, but it has nothing to do with body parts. But he is entitled to his view.

And not only will everybody's mind particle interdigitate with everybody else's mind particle, but you and I and everybody else will travel through computers, absorbing all the information contained in the computers. Your mind particle will travel through a computer, and you'll get all the knowledge in any computer too—such as IBM's Watson, which has beaten people on *Jeopardy*. Maybe it didn't win every time, but it won some of the time.

Everybody's going to know all languages, and therefore, if everybody knows all languages, then it becomes one language, and I call it "mind particle language" or "soul particle language." When they talk in the Bible and all that about getting our bodies resurrected—we will have bodies, but the thing is, your mind particle can grow to any size and shape you want it to be, so you will become your own body and you will not be burdened with an imperfect, problematic body the way you are now. Your mind, brain, soul and body will be a single particulate entity (i.e., particle) that can assume any size and shape you want it to assume.

If you want your body to be exactly like Marilyn Monroe's, then it will be, but it will be just one particle. It won't be that you cut her and she bleeds, no. It'll just be this one particle grown to the size and shape of Marilyn Monroe. So you'll have a body, but it won't be the same as the bodies we have here, where everything can go wrong with them and they are very vulnerable.

# Chapter 69

*Except on planet Earth, everything exists for the sake of pleasure . . . .*

Each mind particle—see, the physicists right now are saying that all matter is made up of these string particles. That's what they are called. So physicists are saying that everything is made up of these little particles that are ten to the minus thirty-three meters long and zero thickness—but they've got to have some thickness, so they can't be right. And one of the biggest questions in physics is, why does anything exist? Why isn't there just infinite empty space and empty time?

The answer is pleasure. Everything exists for the sake of pleasure. Now, here on Earth, we find that's not the case. Here on Earth, the acquisition of pleasures of any kind is pretty difficult, but that's why our planet is special. You have to earn a living. I mean, most people do. I'm on disability, which then makes me feel guilty that I'm not working slavishly the way many people are, and because I feel like dead weight. But I mean, most people have to earn a living, and so that in itself takes away from the idea of somebody saying that everything exists for the sake of pleasure, here on Earth.

Anyone would say, "Well, what great pleasure is here?" But in the universe at large, every pleasure comes easily to that infinite number of mind/soul particles. Each one of those particles comes into existence all for the fun of it—and there is so much fun out there. We're not having it here, and that's why I say we should be able to decide when we want to leave, because life here on planet Earth is hard. Regardless of whether you're earning a living or whether you're an older person whose body is falling apart, life is not that much fun here on Earth. Beyond the confines of Earth (hell), wishful thinking may be realistic thinking.

# Chapter 70

*Even though we are famous, part of the hell of life on Earth is that we're not allowed to know it . . . .*

When you are in heaven, a paradox is that heaven contains the extraterrestrial space aliens, excludees from center-stage earth, who are envious of planet Earth, and yet planet Earth is where the suffering is. So it would seem like it doesn't make sense. If they are in heaven, even though they are not famous, and we're in hell, even though we are famous, part of the hell of it is that we're not allowed to know it.

I mean, we know there are some people who are famous here on Earth—Hillary Clinton, Bill Clinton, whatever—but that's all designed to make us jealous too, because since the infinite number of particles out there in the universe are jealous of us, they are saying, "Let them have a taste of their own medicine." So that's why we have so much injustice as far as the maldistribution of fame, the maldistribution of money, and—let's see, what else is maldistributed? Intelligence or learning ability, good looks, etc.

Fame and money are extremely maldistributed here on Earth, but the reason is that the infinite number of space aliens out there say that if they can be expected to put up with being jealous of our being center stage, then we can put up with jealousy of Whitney Houston, Mitt Romney and/or any other celebrities.

# Chapter 71

## *Except on planet Earth, it's more fun to exist than not to exist . . . .*

Your mind or soul particle can pop in and out of existence, depending upon whether there is pleasure in the environment. Nobody can hurt you in heaven, because if somebody tries to hurt you, all you have to do is either disappear and reappear at some distant location or dissolve into infinitesimally small particle-ettes and get away from them that way.

Either way, it makes sense that the reason a particle pops into existence is because it's more stable to exist than it is to not exist, and pleasure and stability are one and the same thing. So the reason why anything exists in the universe is because it's more fun to exist than not to exist, and being more fun to exist than not to exist means being more stable. So pleasure is the thing that stabilizes us. Pleasure = stability, except in the special case of mind-numbing pleasure such as that induced by alcoholic beverages.

If you think about your own life and the things that give you pleasure, they make you feel stable. Whereas if you think about things that give you displeasure, they make you feel unstable. So, pleasure and stability are basically the same thing, and the reason we don't have just infinite empty space and time is because particles pop into existence all for the fun of it.

And if particles can pop into existence as a particle, as a string particle—ten to the minus thirty-three meters long—then you can go from being small in size to being enormously, even infinitely large. Hence, you can go from being nothing to being ten to the minus thirty-three meters and then grow to an infinite size. If it's not illogical to go from nothingness to somethingness, then it's not illogical to go from something small to something big.

# Chapter 72

*Everybody knows they are going to get their turn to be God in a small universe . . . .*

In larger universes, you have to have suffering, because nobody would pay attention to the central reference point unless it were extremely unique in some way, and so it has to be painful in order to be unique enough to hold the attention of the whole, very large universe. There are very large universes, and there are very small universes. But there is probably only one infinite universe, and we are at the center of it because there are so many problems and so much suffering here.

The very small universes are like small towns. Nobody has to suffer, because everybody knows they are going to get their turn to be

God in a small universe. Each person knows that they are going to get their chance to be God. But in a very large (probably infinite) universe like our universe, there are a virtually or actually an infinite number of mind/soul particles that don't believe they are ever going to get their turn. Even though they are assured by God that they are going to get their turn, they don't believe it.

That's why they are hell raisers. That's why they want to make our lives miserable: because they figure, "Those lucky stiffs—they get to be center stage, and who are we? We're nobody. Nobody knows who we are. We are just this infinite number of nameless people." And so even though God says, "You'll get your turn; you'll get your turn," they don't believe it, because they've been waiting forever to get it and they haven't gotten it yet. Actually, smaller universes make more sense.

# Chapter 73

## *It's like karmic osmosis . . . .*

I realized that everyone has an opportunity to be God because nature is basically fair. Nature is, sooner or later, fair. It's just like—I got a speeding ticket the other day, and I was waiting in line with fifty other people. Most of them were younger people. We know younger people tend to be fast drivers. Everybody just automatically lined up. It didn't matter which gender they were or what color their skin was. Everybody just lined up. It's like, "Yeah, I know you are equal to me and you got here first. You've been waiting longer. It makes sense for you to go ahead of me."

So it's actually part of nature, in particular, a kind of osmosis. In osmosis, you have a semipermeable membrane with particles on either side, and the fluid solvent distributes itself in such a way that the same amount of fluid surrounds each particle. So it's like karmic osmosis. Karma is basically "what goes around comes around," and so if there were one person or even three people who were always superior to the rest of us, it just wouldn't make sense. The universe would become unstable, because power corrupts and absolute power corrupts absolutely. In karmic osmosis, mind particles are analogous to the inanimate particles, pleasure is analogous to water/solution and our brain-body pairs are analogous to the semipermeable membrane.

When it comes to Jesus, I even believe that the wine and the bread can be the blood and body of Jesus. I believe that, because if we're saying everything is made up of super string particles, then it would be possible for the bread and the wine to be the body and blood of Jesus' very large mind particle. When people get a lot of attention focused on them, they tend to grow, even to an infinite size.

Jesus, God the Father, and the Holy Spirit, the three of them having all been elected—their souls grew. They grew because there is a reason for them to grow; so they can have a more powerful size. The three of them arbitrate between us and the angry, jealous, malicious extraterrestrial space aliens, who didn't get included in the Earth's population and never have been to any other previous hell. So the three of them are needed to arbitrate between us and our enemies.

This idea that God the Father would have Jesus crucified just for the hell of it—that doesn't make any sense. What does make sense is that the extraterrestrial space aliens say, "Hey, you guys are just a little bit too big for your britches. Some blood is going to have to get spilled." That makes more sense.

Even the idea of original sin with Adam and Eve in the garden of Eden—basically, Adam and Eve in the garden of Eden is like the extraterrestrial space aliens wanting their turn to be God. It's like, "Okay, Adam, and okay, Eve, you'll get your turns. Just wait. I'm telling you to wait." They couldn't wait; they were impetuous; they wanted to know right now. The story of Adam and Eve is, quite conceivably, literally true, and the bit about the wafers and the wine being the body and the blood, it could be. I mean, anything could be made up of string particles, and the string particle plasma in which they consist.

# Chapter 74

*Pleasure and pain diminution are
really one force . . . .*

Also physicists say there are four essential forces in the universe:
gravity, the strong nuclear force, the weak nuclear force, and
electromagnetism. That's what they say. But on the other hand,
they are saying all matter is made up of string particles. Then, since
matter is condensed energy, and energy is dissolved matter, if they
are saying everything is made up of string particles, then they are
saying there is only one kind of matter.

But since energy is dissolved matter and matter is condensed
energy, then what they are really saying is there is only one form
of energy too. And so the four forms of energy that supposedly

exist—the strong nuclear force, gravity, electromagnetism and the weak nuclear force—are really all one force. And what is that force? Pleasure. Pleasure and pain diminution. If there's only one kind of matter in the universe (and it can either be animate or inanimate, depending on whether its consciousness switch is turned on and to what degree), then there's got to be only one kind of energy, since we know pleasure (and its evil aspect, pain/suffering), it must be the only kind of energy.

Pleasure and pain diminution are really one force, because if you have a pain, you want to relieve it, and if you have pleasure, you want to maximize it. Pleasure augmentation and pain diminution are actually two ends of the same pleasure-pain continuum, which I call PLEPADIM. That's an acronym for pleasure and pain diminution. And so if the physicists are right in saying that there is only one kind of matter, then they are contradicting themselves by saying there are four different forces of energy. And I say if there is only one kind of matter, then since matter is condensed energy and energy is dissolved matter, then there must only be one force, and that force is PLEPADIM. "Force" and "energy" are virtually synonymous in this context.

# Chapter 75

*So the question is whether or not*
*computers are conscious . . . .*

Therefore, inanimate objects experience pleasure. This table that I'm leaning on right now—the particles that make it up are experiencing subconscious pleasure, and that's what holds them together as a table. So the distinction between animate and inanimate is very small but if within a macroscopic object, if you have even one particle that has its consciousizer switch fully turned on, then it's an organism. It's a being. Having the consciousizer only partly turned on is consistent with being an inanimate object which experiences subconscious awareness and pleasure.

So the question is whether or not computers are conscious. A computer will be conscious when and only when and if and only if it contains one particle which has its consciousizer fully turned on. And inanimate objects like your body minus your mind/soul particle (MSP)—like the table that I'm sitting at, the chair that I'm sitting on and computers—are entirely made up of particles that are either unconscious or subconscious, and ones that are subconscious are experiencing pleasure just in being. They take pleasure by vibrating with the other particles around them, so inanimate objects and animate objects are not too far apart. Both kinds of objects are motivated exclusively by PLEPADIM.

# Chapter 76

## *So I recommend small universes . . . .*

We should have small universes, because then we don't have to have any suffering, because everybody knows they are going to get their turn to be God. There are small universes out there, but human nature tends to be greedy when it comes to fame, money, etc. And so that's why there are people living in small universes—there is no suffering there, but they never feel as though they have hit the big time.

Whereas living in an infinitely large universe like our universe is like living in New York City. There is a lot of bad stuff, but there is good stuff in the sense that it's more center-stage, hence more grandiose. So basically original sin is greediness for fame more than money, because in all heavens—in big heavens and small heavens—there is plenty of money. So they don't even need money. Money is obsolete throughout all heavens within all universes, whether they're small, big, or infinitely large as ours is.

In fact, I predict that money will be obsolete right here on Earth by the end of this century. Money will be obsolete because we'll have reproducible out-of-body experiences, and everybody will feel everybody else's wants and needs, and goods and services, which will be effortless and plentiful thanks to pleasurable mind/brain stimulation, will automatically get redistributed. If you and I feel each other's needs and wants, then if I have more money, I'm going to send you some money. This will be because everybody will feel everybody else's wants and needs. So money won't be necessary. Also, pleasurable mind/brain stimulation will render learning and working effortless and intensely enjoyable. Consequently goods and services will also be so plentiful that they won't cost anything and money will be obsolete just as effortful activities will be obsolete.

In heavens in general—whether they are small universes with small heavens or big universes with big heavens—money is obsolete. But greediness for fame is the original sin. Fame and power, the desire to be God—we all have it, but it's a sin. If we would content ourselves to live in small universes where nothing is particularly grandiose, then there wouldn't be any suffering. Everybody would know they're going to get their turn to be center stage as well as their turn to be God.

A finite, small universe is like a small town. If you live in a city even as big as Buffalo and somebody tells you you're going to get your turn to be the mayor of Buffalo, you might not believe it, but if it's a town like the town that my mom grew up in, Warsaw, New York—if you had told her that she was going to get her turn to be the mayor of Warsaw, she would've believed it. It's just a town of four thousand people. So I recommend small universes. Less grandiose but more compassionate small universes—that's what I recommend.

# Chapter 77

## *By the year 2070, we'll be able to take our mind particles out of our bodies . . . .*

All you have to do is get your mind particle out of your body, which will happen, I say, by the year 2070. By the year 2070, each of us will be able to take our mind particle out of our body, and then we will be able to travel anywhere in the infinite universe, and nobody will be able to hurt us. And the upper speed limit will be infinite as opposed to the speed of light.

Let's see. We're in 2012. I'm saying that in fifty-eight years, you might think you're going to be dead, but you will not be. Your mind particle will be around, and your mind particle will be able to go to any other universe at least as a tourist or visitor. You might say, "Well, I'm tired of waiting forever to be God here in this big universe, so I'm going to go to a very small, comfy universe where everybody is on good terms with everybody else. There is no envy, and everybody gets to be God."

So in about fifty years, you'll have a turn to be God in a small place if you want to. You could still come back to a big place like this. Then there will be the issue or question "When will I get my turn to be God?" Well, it's proportional to the infinity of time divided by the infinity of space, but time is infinitely bigger than space, because even though space is infinitely big, it stays the same, whereas there is always more time.

# Chapter 78

*I recommend moving to a small universe*
*and staying there . . . .*

So if I were some authority or even if I were just a friend of yours, and you were to ask me when I think you'll get your turn to be God, I would say, "Well, infinity divided by infinity, that is the likelihood of anyone becoming God which is proportional to the infinity of time divided by the infinity of space." Normally, you'd say, "Well, if it's infinity divided by infinity, then that's one, because anything divided by itself is one," but that's not so.

In mathematics, infinity divided by infinity is undefined unless you know the underlying functions, and there is infinitely more time than there is space, because space is infinite but it's a static, unchanging infinity. It never changes; it never grows. The infinity of space is always the same size, but the infinity of time is always growing, always growing. There is always more time.

So if you ask me when will you get your turn to be God in a big or even infinitely big universe, I'll say, "You'll get your turn sooner or later," and then you'll say, "Yeah, but I might have to wait until an infinite amount of time elapses." And I would say, "That's true, but I recommend moving to a small universe and staying there, being content with just being the God of a small universe, where there is no suffering." That's what I would say.

# Chapter 79

## *This, I think, would be something easier to digest . . . .*

I want to discuss pleasurable brain stimulation because I want to raise consciousness about it. I read about these people in physics, one of whom is Lisa Randall, who asks the question, "Why does anything exist?" and I think I have the answer. So, I would like to send her this short book—and another copy of it to Michio Kaku. He is also a well-known physicist. He may be a little too well known, so when and if I write to him, he might not read the book. But even people who are sophisticated scientifically are going to be more likely to read something short, I would think.

# Chapter 80

## *To me, having an afterlife is a lot more important than having a God . . . .*

I personally think atheists are simple-minded people (at least about theoscience (the interface between religion and science)), even though my mother was one and I was one growing up. I think atheists are theoscientically simple-minded people, and I've got friends who are atheists. I've got this one who loves science-fiction movies, and yet he thinks there is nothing after this life, and I say, "Fact is stranger than fiction," and he says "Yeah, I know."

But it's more like a battle of wills—that he just doesn't want to yield. But some people are on the borderline between atheism and believing in an afterlife. To me, having an afterlife is a lot more important than having a God. Who cares if there is a God? Good for God if there is. I mean, I care about if there is a God, especially whether or not everyone gets a turn, sooner or later. If everyone doesn't get a turn to be God, then it's just one guy or three guys who always dominate forever. Good for him or them. But what does that have to do with me? I don't care.

# Chapter 81

*It's all based on meanness, the meanness of the*
*extraterrestrial space aliens . . . .*

I don't think nature or the universe is so unfair as to favor the three
Trinitarians over everybody else forever, because for every action
there is an equal and opposite reaction. Nature just tends to be equal
and things tend to equilibrate. I hope what I have to say is compelling
enough that some people who are on the borderline between being
atheists and being believers of some sort might be pushed toward
believing, which I think then makes for a happier life. I call the
embittered Earth-excludees "extraterrestrial space aliens" because
they don't live on Earth (hence, "extraterrestrial"), "space" (because
they live in "outer space") and "aliens," because they feel alienated
by virtue of their exclusion from center-stage earth.

I think the whole idea that we die and that's the end of it—I think that is a vicious illusion foisted upon us by the angry extraterrestrial space aliens. Because they are angrily envious, they want us to think that death is something final. Similarly they want us to think (contrary to hypothetical or actual fact) that most of us are not secretly famous throughout the infinite universe and most of us will never be rich, brilliant, etc. They want us to think that we're going to die in a consciousness-terminating way. It's all based on meanness, the meanness of the extraterrestrial space aliens. They really are against us, but if I can say something that undermines what they are trying to do, then I'm happy to say it.

# Chapter 82

## *There is an infinite population of mind particles who have been God . . . .*

One last thing. With every big bang cycle, a new planet gets selected to be the center stage of the universe, but there is an infinite population of mind particles who have been God and are not jealous of the center stage people. So there is an infinite number of alienated angry extraterrestrial space aliens, but there is also a smaller infinity of hell-graduated and godified (having had their turn to be god) mind particles (beings). Some infinities are bigger than others.

The infinity of time is infinitely greater than the infinity of space. In the same way, the infinity of people who have never been to hell, to the center stage of the universe—that number is vastly or infinitely greater than the number of mind particles who have been to hell. So what I'm saying is that among all of that infinite number of mind particles (beings) that are out there, there are some who are not our enemies. Some are not jealous at all, because they've been to hell themselves, and they've been God, so they are not angry or malicious.

# Chapter 83

*Heaven is more logical than not and science and technology will solve all of our problems . . . .*

I hope readers will be persuaded that heaven is more logical than not and that science and technology will solve all of our problems, sooner or later. That sums it up pretty well. Science and technology will solve all of our problems sooner or later, and everyone will get a turn to be God.

Afterthought: What's especially good about Laura is that she has always been a supportive friend, even throughout my periods of severe mental illness. The importance of her support cannot be overemphasized. I love her for her loyalty and reliability.

@@@

QOD1: "I live with this eighty-five-year-old guy whom I love as a person more than I thought anybody could love anybody else."

QOD2: "Having a daughter makes you realize that there is somebody who is, in a sense, more important than you are, because she will be part of the pre-heavenized future."

The recent discovery (by physicists) of the "God Particle," a particle that imparts mass to all other particles, tends to support the mind-soul, physical particle theory of consciousness. According to this hypothesis, if God might be a single particle of matter and you and I are made in God's image, then it stands to reason that you and I also (each of us Earthlings) might be a single particle, albeit temporarily, punitively trapped inside a burdensome, vulnerable body or brain-body pair.

Quantum physics says the value of a computer element can be both zero and one at the same time. More probably, the value is oscillating and/or undulating so fast, perhaps faster than the speed of light, that it is merely an illusion that the value is both 0 and 1, simultaneously. God certainly can move faster than the speed of light, so it may not be an upper limit for anyone or anything, except the relativity equations.

Astrophysical black holes and/or wormholes may be the entrances to the tunnels, whereby mind particles go to Heaven or have out-of-body or near-death experiences.

Dark matter and dark energy are very difficult to detect but comprise some 96% of the universe's mass. Dark energy, which pushes heavenward, and dark matter, which pulls purgatory-ward, might be God and the angry extraterrestrials, respectively. Antimatter and neutrinos might be connected with the latter (the evil ones). And these evil ones might not reside in heaven proper but in purgatory, which might be a realm that is intermediate between hell (i.e., Earth) and Heaven.

Moreover, since dark energy is becoming more dominant and pervasive throughout the universe, it could be God. Since dark matter is becoming less dominant and less pervasive throughout the universe, it could be the devil along with the malevolent extraterrestrials.

In a sequel to this book, such topics as the heaven-purgatory-hell tri-chotomy, as opposed to the simpler heaven-hell dichotomy, and the possibility that the infinite universe actually consists in an infinite number of finite universes might be delved into.

Lastly, the Law of Conservation of matter will probably prove true and correct, because all the matter that will ever exist always has existed and none has ever or will ever be created or destroyed. However, the Law of Conservation of Energy will probably not prove true or correct, because there is always more and new energy being generated and utilized in the form of pleasure and pain-diminution-drive (plepadim).

# Chapter 84

## *You're Just a Particle Trapped inside a Human Brain — Body Pair*

Whenever we feel someone is behaving selfishly, we feel that someone is only concerned about one thing, such as one particle. Hence, the self is just one thing, such as one particle. It is certainly not billions of things, such as brain cells, molecules or even atoms or subatomic particles. As we shall see, your mind is a single subatomic particle that is a string particle.

When we think of the concept of one person, we think of an individual, meaning an undividable one something, such as a particle, as opposed to a brain or a body, both of which are made up of billions of component parts.

As the distinguished psychiatrist and author, Jeffrey M. Schwartz, M.D., together with Rebecca M. Gladding, M.D. have written, YOU ARE NOT YOUR BRAIN, published by the Penguin Group, copyright 2011. Instead, they seem to suggest that you are your mind. It is obvious what and where the brain is, but less obvious what and where the mind is, anatomically- and structurally-speaking.

So if your brain and mind are two different things, your mind may be either too small to be seen (such as a small particle) or it may occupy dimensions of space that we do not have direct access, to, in which case the mind could be large like the golden halos painted around God's, angels' and saints' heads, hundreds of years ago.

Extra spatial dimensions that we cannot touch, feel or otherwise explore with our senses can be understood in terms of string/superstring theory's extra dimensions of space or, more simply, in terms of our discoveries that molecules and atoms are mostly empty (hence, extra) space.

The artists who painted the halo depictions centuries ago did not have an many facts as modern artists, etc. do, but perhaps they compensated for the paucity of facts by overdeveloping their intuition. Hence, they knew/intuited the halos were there even if they couldn't see them. Those halo-sized particles might occupy the empty space in molecules and atoms or extra spatial dimensions which string particles leave empty by dint of their one-dimensional thin-ness (length without appreciable thickness).

And then there are modern psychics and spiritualists, who claim they can see an aura of color and/or waveforms around each person's head. Perhaps they are seeing the mind-soul particle. Out-of-body and near-death experiences wouldn't be expected to yield a bigger-than-halo-sized mind particle, that might temporarily ascend to Heaven.

In 1619, the reknowned astronomer, Johannes Kepler wrote that the "soul has the structure of a point... and the figure of a circle..." Couldn't he have been describing an enlarged and shape-modified string particle/mind particle? He wrote this in Harmonices Mundi.

I have never had an actual out-of-body or near-death experience, but I have heard myself snoring. Hence, my brain may have been fully asleep, while my mind may have been fully awake. Hence, my own firsthand experience may have indicated to me that the mind and brain are two different physical things.

Often when we hear about a plane crash, the announcer will say 100 - some "souls" perished. This, too, indicates that deep within our intuitive subconscious mind, we realize that each person is a single, somewhat solitary something and not a collection of billions of particles.

Your mind is your mind particle (MP), which may also be equated with and referred to as your mind-experiencer-soul particle (MESP). So, "mind", "experiencer", and "soul" may be thought of as synonyms and, therefore, used interchangeably.

Genetics, too, may be overrated. Chimpanzees are much closer and more similar to humans genetically than dogs are. But anyone who has heard stories or witnessed chimps' sometimes barbaric behavior as well as dogs' sometimes compassionate behavior, knows that dogs are more nearly human than chimps are.

Also on the subject of genetics, since identical twins are genetically identical, the differences that exist between them might aptly be explained by there being two different mind-experiencer-soul particles (MESPs) involved.

If you are your brain, then why can severe epileptics have as much as half of their brain's removed and still seem to remain the same MESP? Or, if you're your brain, then why do we generally still feel you're you, i.e., the same person even if you become severely afflicted with Alzheimer's Disease, even when your personality and intellect become unrecognizable?

And if and when we were/will be surgically-advanced enough to transplant half of my brain into interconnection with/up against a remaining half of your brain, that is, the brain in question would be half you/yours and half me/mine, then who would the resulting being be? You, me, half-you, half-me, a drowsy you alongside of a drowsy me that might somehow manage to be a single alert MESP?

Even if you're not convinced that each conscious being is its own MESP, let's assume it for the purpose of the following discussion.

## Reference

1. Schwartz J.M., Gladding R. You Are Not Your Brain. The Penguin Group, 2012, 362 pages, p. 21.

# Chapter 85

*How you might travel anywhere in the infinite universe instantaneously, faster than the speed of light. Plus: Why You're Already a Cosmically Famous Celebrity*

Let's assume that every person's MESP is a particle that is unconscious, semi-conscious/subconscious or fully conscious depending on whether or not and to what degree its internal consciousizer switch is turned on. And every particle is potentially a MESP.

Let's consider the equation.

$$LW = \frac{E}{PA} \times PL, \text{ where } LW = \text{Learning and/or}$$

work(ing) that has been or could be accomplished, E = effort,

PA = performance anxiety and/or pain and

PL = pleasure and/or interest taken in subject matter.

Now, let's consider that PA and PL inhibit each other in a reciprocal way. Hence, $PA = \dfrac{1}{PL}$

By substitution, we get:

$$LW = \dfrac{E}{\dfrac{1}{PL}} \times PL$$

$$= Ex(PL)^2$$

or

$$LW = E \times PL^2$$

Next, we notice that this equation has a similar form to that of Einstein-Poincare's mass-energy relation, $E = mc^2$ where E = energy, m = mass and c = the usual speed of light, which is generally considered to be a constant.

We are aware that as an inanimate object/particle gets close to the speed of light, its <u>mass</u> becomes <u>infinite</u> and it cannot move any faster, no matter how hard you push it/it gets pushed.

But what if the particle were to gradually or suddenly become conscious and make a decision to dissolve into infinitesimally small particlettes of negligible mass, pure, pleasurizing, hence self-propelling energy, or to dissolve into self-propelling nothingness/ empty space/potential energy. Then E (nergy) might become LW, m(ass) might become E(ffort) and $c^2$ might become $(PL)^2 = PL^2$

Then $E = mc^2$ might be replaced by either $LW = E \times PL^2$ or $E = mv^2$, where v = velocity, greater than c, the usual speed of light. Moreover, the velocity of the particle/MESP could ascend to infinity, while the mass would drop to zero (particle dissolved into pure, pleasure-self-propelling energy or temporarily annihilated).

After traveling as far as the particle (such as you) wanted to travel, it could re-condense into a MESP of finite mass. So, anyone could go and come anywhere, no matter how far away, instantaneously.

But how do you consciousize an inanimate/unconscious particle? Perhaps by pleasurizing it with a combination of pleasurable and out-of-body-experience-inducing mind-brain stimulation while it is still lodged in the dog's/person's brain/head, then accelerating it with a combination of particle detectors/accelerators as you launch the MESP out of the brain and into space.

When it has been launched beyond the particle accelerators' realm, with its internal pleasure-sensing switch turned on, it will be so intensely pleasurized that the faster it travels and the more dissolved or temporarily annihilated its matter/mass becomes, the further it will travel. When and if the MESP wants to return to Earth and its brain-body pair, the question will simply be one of self-propelled reversal of direction.

Astrophysicists/astronauts could use some approach such as the above to go and return from <u>any</u> place in the cosmos, instantaneously. The distinguished physicist, Lene/Lena Hau has demonstrated that light can be slowed way down, even stopped. So why can't light or anyone/anything else be speeded up/made to go faster than usual?

The reknowned physicist, Michio Kaku, has said that the discovery of the mass-imparting Higgs boson particle is consistent with the string theory of one-dimensional particles which I believe in. I believe that you are a single $10^{-35}$ meter-long particle, in accordance with string theory's elemental building block theory. You, i.e., your <u>variable-sized</u> but usually $10^{-35}$ meter long MESP are imprisoned inside your brain-body pair.

The observation that so many of nature's equations boil down to elegant simplicity suggests and emphasizes the possibility of intelligent design and de-emphasizes strict creationism, evolution and pure chance.

You have always existed intermittently (flickeringly) and always will. The only sense in which God created you was by assigning you (i.e., your MESP) to the brain-body pair (BBP) in which you find yourself. Since you have existed virtually forever, you have met an infinite number of other MESPs, and they have met and know you. Hence, you are already infinitely famous. Fame and celebrity are somewhat different, but because you have lived on secret center-stage Earth, you are also a celebrity beyond the confines of Earth.

# Chapter 86

## *Equal Everything for Everyone Forever*

Pertaining to the book <u>Does</u> <u>Everyone</u> <u>Get</u> <u>a</u> <u>Turn</u> <u>to</u> <u>Be</u> <u>God</u>, the infinite universe is a democracy rather than a monarchy. And not even Jesus Himself should object to this. There are many reasons why your consciousness must be a single astrophysical particle that is imprisoned for a lifetime within your brain-body pair. And this particle has always and will always interact with every other particle in the universe. Hence, everyone knows everyone else and, consequently, everyone is famous, although the universe is still too jealous to let us know. Everyone gets at least one turn to be God, because everyone is equally special and unique, and there is no better way to celebrate this specialness.

And everyone can travel infinitely fast, because each mind-soul particle (consciousness) can drop its mass to zero, thereby enabling its velocity to ascend to and easily surpass the speed of light. If God can exceed the speed of light, and if everyone is equal to our elected God, then everyone can surpass the speed of light.

# References

1.  Mancini L. S. How learning ability might be improved by brain stimulation. *Speculations in Science and Technology*, 1982; 5 (1): 51-53.

2.  Mancini L. S. Brain stimulation to treat mental illness and enhance human learning, creativity, performance, altruism, and defenses against suffering. *Medical Hypotheses,* 1986; 21: 209-219.

3.  Mancini L. S. Riley-Day Syndrome, brain stimulation and the genetic engineering of a world without pain. *Medical Hypotheses,* 1990; 31: 201-207.

4.  Mancini L. S. Ultrasonic antidepressant therapy might be more effective than electroconvulsive therapy (ECT) in treating severe depression. Medical Hypotheses, 1992; 38: 350-351.

5. Mancini L. S. A magnetic choke-saver might relieve choking. *Medical Hypotheses,* 1992; <u>38</u>: 349.

6. Mancini L. S. A proposed method of pleasure-inducing biofeedback using ultrasound stimulation of brain structures to enhance selected EEG states. *Speculations in Science and Technology,* 1993; <u>16</u> (1): 78-79.

7. Mancini L. S. (written under the pseudonym Nemo Tee Noon, MD). Waiting hopefully. *Western New York Mental Health World,* 1995; <u>3</u> (4), Winter: 14.

8. Mancini L. S. How Everyone Could Be Rich, Famous, Etc., Trafford Publishing, 2006; 240 pages.

9. Mancini L. S. How We'll All be Equally Rich, Famous, Brilliant Etc., Forever, Trafford Publishing, 2010; 190 pages.

10. Kaku, Michio. Hyperspace: A Scientific Odyssey Through Parallel Universes, Time Warps, and the 10th Dimension. Anchor Books, Doubleday, Oxford University Press, 1994, 360 pages: p. 87.

# Two Complementary Compositions

Consistent with the contention that everyone should receive substantial (ideally equal) attention, compositions by two different author-friends have included. Both of my writer-buddies are far more nostalgic than I am, but their nostalgia in no way detracts from or undermines the pervasive futuristic viewpoint. On the contrary, these compositions provide contrast analogously as a black and white painting might be expected to be more interesting than a pure white or pure black painting.

# In Appreciation of Isaac

by Peter G. Runfola

The tongue and lips dance in harmony, as if gliding each syllable through an exquisite Waltz; "Appreciate it," says the South, the words forming a kiss and a smile as the mouth contours to their soft edges.

Like the singsong melody of a belle's beckoning these four syllables (the "A" is silent—'preciate it!) are as southern as mobile aluminum homesteads, the neon contrails of lightning bugs courting potential mates and sweet iced tea on a hot day.

'Preciate it! I defy you to sweat through one day of Carolina heat without this cooling verbal gust of gratitude caressing your ears. Soft and gentle, it floats through the air with the winsome grace of an Autumn leaf.

And like this windblown leaf, subtle hues color the vagaries on the tree of appreciating. In its two truest forms the object 'preciated can range from the vague to the specific, depending on the time frame to which the 'preciating refers. Garnered incrementally, a grand, accumulated collage of debt and gratitude would evoke nothing less than the all-encompassing " 'preciate it." While the more personal response to a certain, time-specific action would justify the lesser-evoked, yet more intimate, " 'preciate that."

Of course, though, as with anything pure and precise, a slang version has evolved from this primordial rubble of syllables. " 'Preciate 'er, son," delivers the immediacy of " 'preciate that," yet talks it walk with a more casual, sauntering gait. Even more personal than " 'preciate that," it relies on the tacit bond between the 'preciator and the 'preciatee to be truly effective. In this hierarchy of gratitude dispensation, " 'preciate that," is Bob, " 'preciate 'er, son," is Bobby. The patriarch of the family, " 'preciate it," still demands the formality of Robert.

Neither is better nor worse nor grander nor lesser a version than the other. They are all sincere incantations of unabashed welcoming of the act which preceded the need to reciprocate a nicety in turn. Together, the triumvirate distill the essence of pure, unadorned symbiosis; all may be seen as demonstrable proofs to the age-old edict that each and every action will in turn spawn an equal and opposite reaction.

When the apple falls from the tree, it will strike the ground with a force consistent with its weight. By analogy, so it is also with the " . . . it, . . . that and . . . 'er, son" triumvirate. Yet it is not the gravity of the 'preciating which they reflect. More, the three connote the intimacy of the 'preciating participants and the time-span encompassed between action and reaction.

Surely, Sir Isaac himself would embrace the crystalline dynamics at work in this elegantly elemental quid pro quo. The variables are few, the equation unencumbered. The three versions remain short and direct, no high-flown verbiage crowding their path from mouth to ear. Like a southern country road they say what they mean and mean what they say; wind your way down Flowes Store Road in Concord and Flowes Store won't be down there but a piece (generations of " 'preciate its" no doubt still lingering in its neglected hull like smiling thought balloons after a cartoonist's convention.)

Like all things southern, this Newtonian triumvirate is poetically poignant, unadorned and succinct. The trilogy are a trio of old country barns whose clapboards have long since lost their love affair with the studs that held them snug—Rubenesque figures both grazing in and feeding into the beauty of a bucolic meadow. Together, they are wildly overgrown bush whose chlorophyll tentacles lovingly hug the rusty skin of the old pickup truck she envelops.

They may serve as closure, as a poetic period when goods are exchanged for money or when a favor is extended. They are elemental. Direct. Yet as eloquent, melodic and all-pervasive as the scent of honeydew on a breezy summer evening.

They are a melodic summer's eve's wafting . . . an oral Mason-Dixon line separating North and South. Listen to the New York (ie. the Southern-perceived capital of the North) version: "Thank You," or the abbreviated, "Thanks," with its misspelled cousin, "Thanx" rounding out the ranks.

Either way, the sound is harsh, grating and nearly as caustic and guttural as New York itself. "Thank you" is the mugger in the slick black raincoat, denying your frantically flying fingernails their half-moon purchases of identifying flesh. It is the bleating of hundreds of taxicab horns, mingled with Iranian curses, holding an impromptu 4 a.m. jam session.

Ahhh, but 'preciating is a symphony. A rhythmic opus evoking the sleep-inducing call of the cricket, the feminine contours of a slim-waisted, large crested curlicue of a road—inscribed into the heart of the forest.

Of course, with the tremendous influx of Yankee blood into the Southerner's homeland, some cross-breeding has occurred. "Thanks, 'preciate it," is one of those rare hybrids that becomes more than simply the sum of its parts. It doesn't reach the magical melding of disparate elements which, say, the Beatles achieved. But it might just have enough of a hook to attain one-hit—wonder status.

Perhaps this is a good thing, this complimentary blending of North and South. After all, it's been a good 130 years since they first kissed and made up.

But, perhaps not. Homogenization tends to leech the flavor from the unique. Usurp power from the different. And if "unique" and "different" begin yielding their individual gaits, their next two-step may be danced in lock step.

No, the South deserves to hold on to its heritage; it is simply different from the North. And different is not implicitly bad, wrong or evil. It is only what it says it is: different.

It is the head and tail which constitute the coin. The ebb and flow of the tides. The yin and yang which, together, create nothing less than the intangible force unifying a universe.

So, blow a kiss and a smile and keep on dancing the dance of the different—and, no matter how you say it: always remember to appreciate.

# The Decline of Cartoons and Comic Books

by James Alan Siggelkow (Inspired by Pastor Godwin)

I was fortunate enough to grow up at a time when the first cartoon that made prime time TV was The Flintstones. This was a clever parody. I remember one particular episode where Wilma and Betty were talking about how modern things were. "Things sure have changed since Thomas Edistone invented the candle". Good, clean, innocent fun.

In today's world, you would not believe the graphic violence and raunchy sex which is shown in today's top cartoons. They're often even sacrelreligious. As far back as the 1930's, someone might get bopped on the head in a cartoon, and there would be a sound effect. That was all. In the next scene, the character automatically bounced back from it, as though nothing happened. That was all.

You didn't see someone get decapitated, with blood spurting out all over the place. This is often the case in today's world. We've always had evil, even in our comic books. But the difference between yesterday and today's world is the fact something was being done about it. People knew when to say HALT!

There was a huge surge of horror comic books in the 1950's. But what was done? They held congressional hearings. Comic books of this type were banned from magazine racks. Each and every comic book had to have a seal of approval put on it before publication. One of the top comic books of today appears in almost a book magazine format. It's much longer than comic books of yesteryear. I wanted to give this comic book a chance so I read three different issues. I lost track of the number of times the "F" word was used. Graphic violence and raunchy sex was often on every page, and sometimes several panels in a row.

But unlike the 1950's, nothing is being done about this. It remains one of the top features out. Isn't it sad that in order to enjoy a truly classic good comic book story, a child has to read one from long ago. The only reason popular titles like Superman, Batman, and Spiderman still exist is because of the prominent reputation they established for themselves in the past. A person can go along time in today's world on past reputation. Put it to the test yourself. Read one of these popular comic books in today's world. Then read one from long ago. I think you'll agree I'm right.

In my kitchen I have comic books covers from 1943; the peak of World War Two. This was when comic books truly deserved admiration. One cover shows, Superman, Batman and Robin throwing baseballs at a poster of Hitler, Mussilni, and Togo. The large caption proclaims, KNOCK OUT THE AXIS WAR BONDS AND STAMPS! Our country reached a zenith of patriotism then we've never seen before or since.

Let's focus on Batman, then and now. You know, the Batman of yesterday's world was a pretty likeable fellow. In spite of the fact he had the grim occupation of fighting crime all the time, he often had a smile on his face. Likewise, the color of his costume, and the various hues of colors, regarding the overall tone of the comic book panels themselves, was cheary and bright.

The Dark Knight of today's world is almost always scowling. It appears he's mad at the world. And rightfully so, considering the point we're at. Likewise, the other characters and colors in today's world of the panels themselves are dark, depressing, gothic! Compare Batman comic book of today's world to one of say, the 1950's. THE DIFFERENCE IS LIKE NIGHT AND DAY! How sad, that in today's world a young child sees in a comic book darkness rather than light; depression and anger rather than happiness.

Indeed, The Dark Knight is a fitting name for a comic book character in today's world. A persons most formative years are their childhood. And one must remember that comic books helps children learn how to read.

I want to say another thing about comic books. Even advertisements in the old days were positive, and often contained a strong "moral" lesson. I recently saw one of these in a comic book dated 1965. It's only one page. It centers around schoolchildren. A retarded or certainly slow child named Todd draws something the other kids make fun of. He runs sobbing out of the room. The teacher informs the others about Todd's handicap. "Gee", they exclaim. "We didn't know. We'll try to help". The last panel shows us that Todd's drawing skills have improved. The last panel and word balloon is another child with his arm around Todd exclaiming, "Gee Todd, that's pretty good. Soon, you're going to have to help us". I have seen many modern comic books and they just would not run something like this today. Believe me, they just DON'T! We have become more callous and insensitive over the years. This is further proof of it!

I'm convinced that Satan's main lure for children reading modern day comic books is the strongest element of the comic book itself:

The Artwork. Many modern comic books are produced and drawn in a very high tech computerized fashion. One panel might show a man getting shot with a gun and have blood spurting-out all over the place. Another panel may depict a woman getting slapped around by an abusive husband.

And yet, this negativity will probably often be overlooked when a child sees it and exclaims, "Wow! Look how well this is drawn! Look at the cool shading techniques and colors employed to achieve this effect? Seeing as how I like to draw, I'll have to buy more issues of this!" Many modern comic books often have a large staff of people working on them. Taking this into account, we should certainly be able to expect more of a positive nature about them.

When comic books first made the scene in the 1930's, there was much more simplicity to them. Often only two people did the whole thing. One would write the stories, while another drew it. I know this was the case in Superman's early days. Good guys fought bad guys. It was often that simple. The stories themselves were often what many would today term "crude". The artwork was often cruder! And yet, there's something about those early comic books of the 1930's that for all their simplicity and crudeness, puts them head and shoulders above the dry, empty (often evil) products of today!

# Siggelkow's Introduction

as written by Nemo T. Noon

The following letter and composition by James Alan Siggelkow illustrate (1) Newton's Third Law of Motion (for every action, there's an equal and opposite reaction), (2) The Second Law of Thermodynamics (heat (like pleasure/happiness) flows from those who have a great deal of it to those who do not), (3) the principle of karma, i.e., "What goes around, comes around," and (4) osmosis, whereby the concentration of solvent tends to equilibrate between high and low solute concentration volumes. In other words, this essay is about unequal situations evolving into equal ones. Therefore, they are relevant and complementary to this book.

Dear Dean,

I can't thank you enough for the wonderful, enlightening impact your letter had on me. I've read it and reread it many times. It was three pages long. But two lines in particular truly saddened and angered me at the same time: "There was a time period when I felt as though I was a failure when it came to being your therapist. Being a positive force in so many other peoples lives relieved me of my guilt, and I would forgive myself for not being able to bring about healing responses in you".

I guess I had some of that coming, in light of how negative and extremely immature that last journal of mine was. I shared some, but certainly not all of your sentiments. Boy oh boy! If I don't redeem myself after reading this essay, I'll be amazed. If you don't redeem yourself after listening to it, I'll also be amazed.

Otherwise, we're both failures!

Sincerely,
James Alan Siggelkow

# The Power of Time, Memory, Resentments, and Rage

by James Alan Siggelkow

As a ten year old child, I found it virtually impossible to even fathom a statement made by adults such as, "that was twenty years ago, but it seems like just yesterday". To me, that enormous length of time would seem dark and dim, with little or virtually no recall.

I'm 58 years old. In some respects, the whole decade of the 1970's seems like a mere eyeblink away. Things like clothing I wore back then, or cars I owned at that time, exist in my memory with sharp detail. It's almost like I could walk out to my driveway today, see a car I owned in 1979, and start driving it as though a mere day, and not thirty plus years had elapsed. As a ten year old, this type of thinking would be totally beyond my perception.

This kind of memory regarding time is quite safe and almost nostalgic. It's also quite scary, when you truly take into account how fast time marches on. When carried into emotional areas such as resentment and rage, time and memory can indeed truly become a terrifying nightmare.

Dave is a close personal friend of mine. He is a kind, polite, gentle, sensitive soul. We share a common interest in nostagic things such as old comics and old movies. We've spent many happy hours enjoying these things together. Dave has a good sense of humor. He makes me laugh.

If he were angry at someone, deeply angry, I would feel that the person who bore his wrath must have treated Dave with unspeakable horror. Dave had told me on several occasions of a person he deeply disliked.

When he used such terms as "the old neighborhood," in describing the era in which he knew this person, I had to conclude it was something which took place a long time ago. I didn't know how long. He told me he suffered much humiliating sadistic physical and verbal abuse from this person.

Moreover, he said the guy had frightfully tortured his pet cat, whom he held in deep affection. One day, my curiousity got the better of me. I asked him, when did the situations you mention with this person take place? For that matter, when was the last time you even saw him? What year? His response? 1965.

He heard "through the grapevine" that this man's sister still lived in "the old neighborhood." He was also informed that his former enemy sometimes came to visit her at this address. One day, he became extremely enraged and went to her house. She was there, but her brother wasn't. Dave said he wished to see him sometime. That was all. And then he left.

When he told me about this, I remembered things you said to me in your letter. I reiterated some of these thoughts to Dave. "Dave, I have sympathy for what happened to you as a teenager. And yes, a great deal of empathy as well. Because what happened to you also happened to me. It happened to me far more than once. In a crazy way, you might say that I'm even still on your side with this thing.

"But the fact of the matter is David, is that you have not known or even seen this person since 1965! Please have some semblance of sanity about it in this respect. He may have mended his ways. He may have stayed the same and just got older. Maybe he got worse. You don't know this, and neither do I. They have a criminal justice system which deals with the actions of juvenile delinquents and criminal adults. It's an organization far bigger than you or I put together. They also have a Humane Society, which justly deals with the abuse suffered by your poor unfortunate cat. Don't do something you'll regret David. Please don't". There's no complete telling if my words penetrated Dave's sanity. It may be today, or many years from now. Time alone will provide the answer . . . Time alone.

The next person I'm going to talk about is a woman named Kay. She was an old lady in her eighties and nineties when I knew her. Kay was a legend in the heaven sent fellowship known as Alcoholics Annoymous. She was a legend because of the enormous amount of time she had without a drink.

She had not taken a drink of alcohol since about 1951. But one would never have known this by the way she conducted herself. I rarely if ever heard her say a kind word about anybody or anything. She was so antisocial, that sometimes, they even had to call the police on her at AA meetings and escort her out. That's how out of control her rage got. She reminded me of a three year old, having a temper tantrum.

Kay once told me her story. She was an only child. Her mother was 40, and her father was 50 when she was born. She seemed to imply that they were more like doting grandparents than parents. Kay grew up in great wealth. In her youth, she was also very pretty. From about the age of 16 on, Kay began not only entering, but winning many beauty pagents. By the time she was a young woman in the

1930's and '40's, she became one of the top models in Buffalo. Her photograph graced the covers of many magazine and routagervere Sunday supplements. She was probably more stable back in those days. I don't know for sure. I didn't know her then. One day, I made the mistake of giving Kay a ride home from an AA meeting. Nothing I said of a consoling nature even diminished one particle of her feelings of livid revenge against one of her many ex husbands.

Her face became so contorted with rage, and her body shook so violently at the mere mention of this man's name, that one could swear that he sat right beside us. Right then! Right now! I therefore felt compelled to ask Kay, "Just out of curiosity, when did the situation you're referring to take place? For that matter, when was the last time you even saw this man? What year?" This was her answer. 1947.

Many people have sometimes responded to Kay in a compassionate way. But there's also something known as a point of no return. I don't know if the situation mentioned about her ex husband was his fault or her fault. But with all due respect, you can not reasonably expect a whole AA meeting to sadly gravitate to her side and say words to the effect of. "We're in full sympathy with you Kay. Even if this thing did happen in 1947".

Kay had me over to her house one day. She proudly got out her old modeling portfolios, and boastfully told me about many of the photographs. I went home and related the experience to my mother. "Gee Mom, it was pretty neat seeing all those old pictures of Kay in her heyday. You know what a nostalgia buff I am. I also enjoyed reading the old newsstories of that time period. For that matter, some of the old advertisements even caught my attention. They were very dated now, but interesting nevertheless."

My mother exclaimed, "Yes Jim, I suppose it was interesting for you to see those things. And I suppose in a way, there was also a mixture of happy and sad nostalgia for Kay as well. For a very brief time, so long ago, she could see herself as she once looked-young and beautiful. But when you come right down to it Jim, what was her main motivation in showing you these things all about? It was all about Kay wasn't it?"

Not long after this, I went to an AA meeting. A common theme which comes up at these meetings is the topic of resentments. On this particular day, people around the table voiced their severe dislike toward an "old timer" in AA by the name of Kay. Many agreed, she seemed to usually have a very negative aura about her. They came to a woman named Helen. Helen remarked, "Poor Kay used to be very young and beautiful. And look at her now-an old wrinkled up woman in her nineties." Then she almost wept.

They came to me, and this is what I had to say. "You know Helen, I recently resaw the movie, "The Elephant Man". Kay grew up in great wealth. God also blessed her with stunningly drop dead good looks. The Elephant man was poor, and would never win a beauty prize for his outward appearance. The Kay I've always known has never been a nice person. But the elephant man was portrayed as a very sweet, kind, gentle, and nice person. And the irony of it is Helen, he had a lot less to be nice about.

"So I can't waste my tears of pity on Kay. Old age is just a fact of life. We can handle it with dignity or bitterness. Kay made her choice". Helen said nothing. What could she say? Up to the day of her death last year at the age of 95, Kay remained a spiteful, bitter, angry person. Much of this hostility was over things that happened in the long dead past. She died in the hospital, and she died alone.

I'm told that the doctors, nurses, and all who knew her remarked that they had never met a more angry, self centered, hostile bitch in all their life!

Kay has been gone for about a year now. Whenever people evoke her name, the most common sentiments expressed are words to the effect of, "I hated that old hag! I hope she rots in hell!" I can't share these feelings. On the contrary, I feel quite sorry for her. I'm not her final judge. But I do somewhat hope that she's in a better, more peaceful place now. Lord only knows, she sure was unhappy in this life.

The last case history I'm going to tell you about is by far the hardest. It's the hardest because I knew him the best. It's also by far the most shocking, because it clearly illustrates how having rage and living in the past can produce the most horrific consequences.

As a child, many of us have a best best friend. We bond to this person like glue. In some cases, we spend more time with this person than we do our own brother. Once upon a time, I had such a person in my life. His name was Larry. From the age of eight to thirteen, we were virtually inseparable. Many weekends, either he would stay at my house, or I at his.

Larry could be very domineering. I didn't like that about him. But the fact remains, I have very pleasant overall memories concerning him and our childhoods. Certainly one of the most pleasant recollections I have of him, is when the two of us built a treefort together at my parents farm in Ellicottville. This was in fifth grade. Many a pleasant day was spent up there, eating peanut butter sandwiches, and reading our comic books. After 44 years, that treefort remains stationed high up in that tree, to this very day.

Larry and I both stopped attending Park school after eighth grade. At that point in time, neither of us were driving yet. Unlike public schools, where most people live a short distance away, at the private school Larry and I attended, kids came from near and far. Larry lived on Grand Island. That's a long way away from Buffalo when you're a kid, and not driving yet.

In spite of our closeness, we lost touch for many years. Then in the early '80's, I started attending AA meetings in Buffalo. I ran into Larry at one of them after many years. He seemed very angry about something. I didn't know what. He admitted he was quite unstable. He confessed to having numerous hospitalizations for emotional problems. Therefore, it would not have surprised me were I to hear that something of this nature were to have happened again.

But never in a million years, was I prepared to face the horror and shock which confronted me one day when I picked up the newspaper. One of the articles read, "Man Charged With Killing His Father". I only had to read the first sentence to know it was Larry. My best childhood friend! According to the article, the police asked him what is probably a very common question: "Why did you do it?" Larrys cold response was, "He beat me!"

The officer was aghast! "He must have been referring to his childhood! Because the murdered man we saw was in no condition to beat anyone! He was a short, wizened, shriveled up old man in a wheelchair. An invalid". Larry by contrast was a great big strapping fellow, well over six feet tall, and almost thirty years old. My parents sadly reflected, "Larry probably got drunk, and thought of some time his father beat him when he was ten. Then he flipped out and killed him."

I know for a fact that to strangle someone, you have to have not only rage, but volcanic rage! I'm told the neck muscle is very strong. Sometimes you have to give it all you've got for a full minute or two to accomplish the task. Larry's cool reception to the arresting officer, was in sharp contrast to the photograph which appeared of him in the newspaper a short time later. Never in my life have I ever seen such an intense mixture of horror, shock, and grief on any one man's face. You could almost hear Larry scream, "My God! What have I done?!" Even in a black and white photograph, you could almost see meloncholy seep from his pores.

Dean, I must have looked at that picture, and read the accompanying article to myself over and over, hundreds of times, until the words just flowed together. I went to see him a short time later at the Holding Center. I didn't know what to say. What can you say? Don't worry. It's not that bad", Throughout his sobbing (which was continous and non stop) he almost meekly asked me several questions. "Jimmy, will you visit me in prison?"

"Yes".

"Will you write me?"

"Yes".

"Will you take my phone calls?"

"Yes. I'll do all that and more, old friend. I'll do the whole shot. You represented a very special time capsule of my childhood. I can't forget that. I won't forget that. I'll never forget that."

As I said earlier, Larry was a big part of my childhood. He was also a big part of my whole family's life for five years. My parents and brother knew him well. It therefore only makes sense, that he appears in many old family home movies. The fifth grade play. Sledding together. Crystal beach. These images are all there, forever perserved on sixteen millimeter film. I haven't seen those movies in years. I suppose if I wanted to temporarily transport myself back in time, I could watch those films and do so. Today I choose not to. I can't speak for tomorrow because it's not here yet. No school paper I ever got an A+ on compares to the mental and spiritual gratification I received while writing this essay.

I recently read a page of a spirtual magazine. In the past, I would have just been reading words with no meaning. Today I can comprehend these words, and I can also apply it. It cites Psalm 51: "Create in me a clean heart, O God; and renew a right spirit within me." The narrator offers his insights, and I heartily agree with them:

"This Psalm caused me to do some deep thinking in the days that followed. How is it with my upstairs-my mind? What things do I keep stored there? Are they valuables in the sight of God, or is it mostly trash such as wrong attitudes, petty grievances, selfishness, wrong motives, and hurt feelings? Are we willing to get rid of this trash, or do we enjoy wallowing around in it? Too often we hang on to these thoughts, thinking they have some value. In reality, they are cluttering space that God would like to occupy. Why not give God the broom and let him do the cleaning?"

Oh Dean! Dean! How can you possibly have any guilt, or think yourself a failure as my therapist, when you take into account the fact that a recent three page letter you sent me, inspired me to write an essay like this. I don't know if anything I've said helped you or not. Indeed, I don't know if you could pass this on to one or many of the people you help, and that in turn could help them some more.

But I Do know one thing for sure. It helped me to write this essay, and for that I'll remain eternally grateful! Thank you, dear friend, and may God bless you!

# Epilogue

This tragic study of these three unhappy lives now comes to an end. Hopefully for me, it signifies a beginning. I don't wish to stay "stuck" anymore, because I don't want to end up like them. Thank God, one of them still remains a question mark. Tragically for two of them, it became too late!

# A Truly Great Man

## 1918 – 2014

Today I pay tribute to a wonderful man. Theodore Roosevelt, one of our greatest Presidents, called his father, "the greatest man I ever knew". These are certainly the same sentiments I have concerning my Dad. President Roosevelts greatest legacy was conservation. We have many of our national parks thanks to him. And yet, he had a strange bloodlust for one so devoted to nature. He thought nothing of killing an animal just for the mere sake of putting its head above the fireplace.

Thank God, my father vastly differed from TR in this respect. Dad was so loving toward all forms of life, that he wouldn't or couldn't, kill so much as a bug or insect without forever feeling guilty about it. Indeed, this is truly a testimony to what a kind hearted man he was.

Second grade was a very noteworthy year for me. I discovered Beethoven, Curious George, and most importantly perhaps, comic books. Dad had always been a big fan of the Sunday comic page. In 1965, he appeared on a half hour TV show on channel 17 concerning this topic. That's how knowlegable he was about comics. I'm sure it was his enthusiasm about the Sunday comic page that initially sparked my interest in comic books.

Second grade was also the first year I got an allowance. Week after week, Dad gave me a franklin fifty cent piece. This is my first vivid memory of any kind of currency I could call my own. Sometimes, he'd give me two quarters instead. I was disappointed about this. He'd exclaim, "But it's the same amount Jimmy. And you're going to spend it anyway".

"I know Dad, but I like having that one large coin in my pocket. It makes me feel like a big shot".

"Well, lets see..." He'd fish around in his pocket, and usually produce the desired coin. That fifty cent piece went quite far in 1963. I could buy a bottle of pop, hostess cupcakes, nickle and penny candy, and one, two, or sometimes three comic books. They were twelve cents then. Sometime ago, I went to the coin store and bought a franklin fifty cent piece from 1963. I look at it quite often. It's the most plesant artifact I have, and a very cheerful reminder of when I was seven years old.

A very prominent man in Buffalo recently informed me, "When I was a college student at UB, your father was so good to me. He was the best Dean Of Students UB ever had!". This person knew Dad when we first moved to Buffalo in 1958. When I brought his name up to my father, Dad humbly remarked, "Gee, I didn't do anything for that guy".

I think Dad was referring to things like helping this man with his career. What Dr. Wolin had in mind were things like Dad the teacher. Dad who took him out to lunch. Dad who joked around with him. Dad the friend. To this very day, well over half a century later, Dr. Wolin is still deeply touched by these memories.

When Dr. Wolin told me this, he had a very sober expression. His face also generated honesty and gratitude. Not long afterward, I saw Dr. Wolin again. Only this time, my father was with me. When Dr. Wolin caught a glimpse of Dad, he bolted up from his chair. With a warm, firm, grateful handshake, and a smile so huge it lit up the sky, he exclaimed, "Dr. Siggelkow!" Then, he said the same thing he'd said to me not long before. Only this time, he said it in front of both of us. "Your Dad was the best Dean Of Students UB ever had!"

I asked the two of them when was the last time they'd seen each other. They reflected for a moment, and concluded it had to be sometime around 1962. Dads all time favorite movie is a holiday classic. With the exception of <u>The Bible</u>, this story helped brighten and bring magic to the full meaning of Christmas like nothing else. <u>All</u> great Christmas movies are an offshot of this one. This was the first. Charles Dickens first penned this classic in 1843.

I'm sure you all know I'm speaking of <u>A Christmas Carol</u>. We meet a mean old miser, who hates everybody and everything. He loves money and nothing else. But it wasn't always this way. The ghost of Christmas past takes him to a party many years before. When Scrooge spots his first employer, it's the first time in the whole movie we see him smile. But what a joyous smile it is! He beams with pleasure at the sight of old Fezzywig.

Happily, he confides to the spirit, "Was there ever a kinder man!" It's a very low key affair. They're not drinking champaign and eating cavair. On the contrary, they're all having a very humble good time just being themselves. The spirit points this out to Scrooge. "And yet, what would a party like this cost in your mortal money? Hardly anything. Is that so great he deserves your praise?"

"Oh, but it wasn't about that", Scrooge answers. "The love, joy, and happiness he brought me and all who knew him were as great as if it had cost...a fortune". My Dad didn't bring Dr. Wolin material wealth. But of far greater importance, be bestowed kindness and compassion along the way which Dr. Wolin never forgot! And the degree of kindness and compassion Richard Siggelkow carried within his heart has no pricetag!

There were so many Dr. Wolins in Dads life. Students, faculty, and staff alike thought the world of Dad. Many students in particular regarded him as a second father. Their fondness for him was demonstrated by the fact they dedicated the UB yearbook, The Buffalonian to him three times throughout the decade of the 1960's-1960, 1964, and 1969.

I'm sorry to say Scrooge took a turn for the worse! As he becomes more ruthless and money hungary, he drives poor Fezzywig out of business. But he docs repent later and has a spiritual experience. I'm glad. I think we were all kind of rooting for him at the onset. Although I must confess, I never met a meaner s.o.b. in my life! (I had to get that in!)

I recall a recent church service I attended with my father. At one point, I looked at him, and he looked at me, and he smiled. It was a smile which generated such kindness, gentleness, senstivity, and love. Several times a week, I go and workout at UB's gym, Alumni Arena. On the way to and from the gym, I pass a building called, "Center For Tomorrow".

In 1983, we held a retirement dinner there for Dad. Thank God, Robert Bodkin suggested we record this event. I can hear it over and over again and never get tired of it. Equality was one of many strong traits of my fathers. Cruelty and discrimination were terms which just didn't exist for him. He had a history of hiring more minorities and handicapped people than most people did in his high profession. He didn't do this to receive praise from anyone. It's just the natural way he was.

His secretary Mildred Holflick summed it up well when she stated, "You will find no predjudice or discrimination in this man. He is as deeply interested in the personal lives of the counter girl in the cafeteria, the waitress in the Tiffin Room, the filling station attendant, the work study assistent in the office, or the new employee who has just joined the staff. He is truly a humanitarian-a great equalizer".

An old army buddy, Amedo Duke, closed his talk with these words: "I'd just like to say that Dicks life can be characterized with dedication, inititive, character, kindness, sentimentality, intuitiveness. gratitude, greatness, enthusiasm, love, knowledge, objectivity, and willingness, and that is Dick Siggelkow". In a very real, clever, and symbolic way, he spelled out Dads name when paying tribute to him.

Larry Smith is a very dear old friend of the family. Throughout the 1960's, he was Dads right hand man. Many times throughout the years, Larry told my mother, "I would do anything for Dick. Anything,"

Indeed, that's the kind of love and loyalty Richard Siggelkow inspired in those who knew him best. Tony Lorenzetti and Elliott Zolin are also dear old friends, who are more like members of the family. I've been thinking alot lately about Dads many years at UB, and all the lovely people he knew and worked with.

But there are two names that stand out above all the rest: Larry Smith, and Tony Lorenzetti. Larry was like an older brother to Rick and I growing up. Larry said a very sweet thing about the entire Lorenzetti family. It's such an honest statement, I have to share it with you tonight. He said, "If you don't love the Lorenzettis, then there's something wrong with you!" In a similar vein, the loyalty of Elliott Zolin can't be matched.

I truly wish to believe with all my heart that when we die, we become reunited with loved ones who have passed on before us. I often heard Dad remark, "My father was the greatest man I ever knew". Dad adored his father, whom he held the deepest affection for. Many of Dads wonderful traits were mirrored and inherited from his father.

For a number of years, I had a bad drinking problem. Through the grace of God, I've been a grateful and active member of a heavensent fellowship known as Alcoholics Annoymous for over three decades. When I first started going to AA meetings, Dad gratefully remarked,

"I'm so proud of you Jim. And I know my father would have been proud too. The three of us".

That was so nice and sentimental - "the three of us". In a sense, it was a double compliment to me. I knew my Dad was proud of me, and my grandfather would have been. I never saw my father drunk in my life, nor did he drink much at all. Both he and mother set a wonderful example in this respect. I began getting into it as a teenager, and got carried away.

My grandfather knew many prominent people, and had the opportunity to rise to high political status, had he so desired. Wealth and fame could have been his. But instead he chose to run on the Prohibition ticket, because like dad, he held steadfast to his convictions. My grandfather died essentially pennyless. And yet, I've read and been told that his service in Madison Wisconsin was truly something to see. Madison was a very small town, and yet hundreds came. The Scroder funeral home was literally jammed packed to an overflow capacity crowd. The people in attendence there that day ranged in stature everywhere from the Mayor to the skid row bum.

And I truly think that speaks volumes about the man and his character. He loved people from all walks of life, and they loved him. But the same can be said about my father. My Dad died much older than my grandfather was. Many of the people Dad knew are gone now. When my grandfather died, an article appeared in the newspaper aptly entitled, "Madison Loses A Landmark".

Today I lost a landmark in my life. But I am filled with a treasure trove of beautiful memories, which I will cherish for as long as I live. I only shared a fraction of those memories with you tonight. Thank you dear father and friend, and may God bless you!

# A Remarkable Woman

## 1922 – 2014

Today I pay tribute to a wonderful person. That remarkable woman is my Mom. She worked hard all her life. The word "sloth" just didn't exist for Lois Siggelkow. She was totally on her own since the age of 17. My mother kept up two large homes, and worked full time. Her occupation was Home Economics.

And boy, could she cook! Her deserts alone were something to rave about! When I was growing up, there would sometimes be more than one in the refrigerator at the same time. I would often remark, "You know Mom, that boston cream pie you baked gave me good dreams for two weeks!"

Her favorite students were seventh grade boys. She fondly recounted to me how they'd run in the room and exclaim, "What are we going to do today Mrs. S.?" Mom would tell them and they'd reply,

"Outstanding!" These students were so happy and excited to be in Moms class. One certainly got the impression they were very fond of her. I know she adored them.

Mom cooked not only on a large scale, but HUGE scale! In the early years of marriage, she cooked for Dads parents, grandmother, brother, sister, nephews, nieces, in laws, etc. Often, all at once! We have an old 1947 recording made at Thanksgiving. Everyone interviewed on the record talked about what a superb meal they had. Justifiably so.

Later on, when Dad became a very successful college administrator, she had big dinners for faculty, staff, etc. Another thing that stands out about my mother is her wonderful sense of history. She did a lot of work researching the original occupants of our home in Ellicottville. But her biggest pet project was the cemetary. This was on our land in the country. Many old stones which were ruined by age and decay were reserected as well as possible.

Once again, she did a lot of detective work concerning the history of the people buried there. We had two major rededication ceremonies there. One in 1976, and another in 1981. She also appreciated her fathers sense of history as well. She recounted how as a sick young boy, he told her he was once fed medicine on a wood chip. That same doctor later developed a cure for yellow fever.

Another memory about my grandfather my mother remembered was the election of President Grover Cleveland. If they heard two shots from a cannon fired in town, this meant that a Democratic victory was assured. Rick and I have always been very proud of the fact that there was a good degree of native american blood on my mothers side of the family. We have a classic photograph of my grandmother at eighteen, dressed in full Indian regalia.

Mom grew up on a farm in the 1930's. That's why she could appreciate a TV show like "The Waltons". It shows a close family like hers was, as well as depicts what the depression was like. In her youth, Mom was exposed to all kinds of different animals. She loved them all. She and her sister Barbara even made personel pets out of the cows. But there was a special place in her heart for cats.

She adored them! Sometimes the neighbor would over hear her talking to our beautiful orange Persian cat on the porch. It was as though "Kitty" were a real person, and not just an animal. Some people may feel this was silly. I think it was sweet and cute.

My parents and I had a nice tradition going in recent years. Every Friday we had dinner together, and then we'd go to my place and watch old television reruns of "Leave It To Beaver". This was nostalgic for us all. My parents remember watching that show when they were much younger, and I recall it being one of the first programs I saw as a child.

My mother was the kind of person who said what she thought, and meant what what she said. We were watching one episode where Lumpy admired himself in the mirror. As he gazed upon his reflection he exclaimed, "You doll!" My mother honestly responded, "Lumpy is a big lump of crap!" Lumpy paid alot of rent in that dream world he lived in.

It's a shame a show like this is now referred to as "classic" TV, and not "current" TV. Putting the humerous aspect aside, there were often good morals on shows like this. Be honest. Don't hurt someones feelings. We just don't have programs like that anymore. Thank God for DVD's. And thank God my mother always retained those values herself.

One of my most pleasant childhood memories concerns my mother, brother, and myself when I was about four. The three of us went to a function at my brothers school, and on the way home got lost. We cut across a big field that was very deep with snow. We all kept falling down, and laughing in the snow. We were lost, but it didn't matter. We had so much fun just being together-laughing and falling in the snow.

This is the way I remember Mom the best-laughing and enjoying life. Thanks for the memories Mom. You truly were a remarkable woman!